YOU RULE!

Create Your Own Country

YOU RULE!

Create Your Own Country

Contents

Pick a place

Homeland	08
Expand your horizons	10
Up for grabs	12
Small is beautiful?	14
Who needs land?	16
Worlds beyond	18

Mark your territory

Shaping up	20
Border security	22
Looks good on paper	26

Make it official

What's in a name?	28
Ready to fly	30
Herald a new nation	32
Declare yourself!	34
Making the grade	36

Bring a crowd

Come visit!	38
Stay forever!	40
Life members	42
Settling in	44
Getting cozy	46

Show who's boss

Going solo	48
Power sharing	50
Dicing with democracy	54
Vote winning	56
Staying in control	58

9001109775

Get down to business

Make money!	60
Resource rich?	62
Making dough	64
National networks	66
To the letter	68
Keep them coming	70

Dress it up

Look the part	72
Get some culture	74
Sing your country	76
Time out	78

Troubleshooting

National security	80
Love thy neighbor?	82
You and whose army?	84
I'll scratch your back	86

Pass it on

Preparing the way	88
All thanks to you	90

Glossary   93

Index   94

Introduction

Tired of where you live? Ever thought you could organize things better? Well, now's your chance! This book will show you how to create your very own country, from scratch. You'll work out where to place it, what to call it and how many people should live in it. You'll get to decide, organize, govern and judge. You can choose to be king, queen, big chief, emperor or president. Because from here on, in your country, *you* rule!

Of course, you won't be the first to set up a country. People have founded dozens of new ones over the centuries. And in recent years many individuals and groups have created their own unofficial states, known as micronations. None of these have been recognized by other, official countries. But that hasn't prevented them continuing to exist—or stopped their rulers having fun!

So join in and start planning. And don't worry: if the decisions get too much for you, there are tips and quizzes in these pages that will help you make up your mind and keep you on the path to righteous rule and the endless adoration of your subjects. Plus you'll learn how to think up placenames, draw a map of your country, design your own flag, crown, stamps and coins, and lots more.

Ready to rule? Then throw on your robes, dust off your crown—and start nation-building!

Pick a place

First you've got to decide where your country is going to be. Of course, you normally need land—and quite a lot of it—for a country. Unfortunately, most land on Earth is already claimed. And, yes, that's a bit of an obstacle, but don't let it put you off. Size isn't everything and, as many people have shown, as long as you're inventive, you'll find a place to call your own.

Homeland

If you want to keep things simple, create your country in part of your home. That way you're on territory your family already holds. You could even start a country in your room! True, it doesn't allow for much expansion, and it could be a bit of a squeeze if anyone else wants to join in. But, on the up side, it can be a good way of keeping pesky brothers, sisters and parents out of your nation's affairs. And, hey, you might not even have to get out of bed!

Keep out!

Reach out

Setting up a micronation at home doesn't mean you can't get other people involved. In 1979, 14-year-old Robert Ben Madison created a kingdom in his room in Milwaukee, USA. He called it Talossa, from a Finnish expression meaning "inside the house" and named himself King Robert I. After he created a Talossa website in the late 1990s, people all over the world applied to join his country (while continuing to live in their own rooms, of course). Today, Talossa has about 250 "citizens" worldwide.

Garden state

If you're more of an outdoors type, then your nation could be born in your own backyard. Ask your parents if you can claim part of the garden for yourself. That's what 15-year-old Australian George Cruickshank did in 1981. He named his 108 sq. feet (10 sq. meters) of backyard in the suburbs of Sydney the Empire of Atlantium. About 3,000 people have since joined the empire, which now includes a larger property outside Sydney.

WELCOME TO
THE EMPIRE OF ATLANTIUM
ATLANTIUM

Stake your claim

If you're running out of options, try a land grab—just be bold and claim somewhere. Why not a corner of that park down the road, or that stretch of woods that no one seems to use? Hundreds of years ago, this worked very well. In 1513, for example, explorer Vasco Núñez de Balboa reached the west coast of Panama in Central America and immediately claimed the entire Pacific Ocean and all lands adjoining it for Spain! Similarly, in 1770, Captain James Cook claimed the whole east coast of Australia for Britain, even though he knew Aboriginal people were already living there. Cheeky, huh?!

Expand your horizons

Maybe there's no land available locally. Or you'd just like something more exotic—a seaside principality, perhaps, or a cute little island state? It's time to look further afield. Get out your atlas, check online maps, scan the globe and see what you can find...

Dots on the map

Islands are always appealing, and there are thousands of them out there. Most belong to larger nations, but look hard and you never know what you might find. In 1996, Gregory Green spotted an island in the Pacific Ocean that appeared to have no owner, so he quickly declared it the New Free State of Caroline. Sadly for Gregory, the island was officially granted to the real Pacific state of Kiribati a few years later.

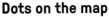

Writers' realm

In 1865 Matthew Dowdy Shiell, an English trader living in the West Indies, worked out that no one had claimed the tiny uninhabited island of Redonda, near Antigua. So he proclaimed himself king and passed the title to his son, Matthew, who later became a novelist. Matthew junior, or King Felipe I as he styled himself, passed the title in turn to another writer, John Gawsworth, aka King Juan I. Mystery surrounds what happened after Gawsworth's death, and today several men from different countries, mainly writers, claim to be King of Redonda. In the kingdom's history, however, only two kings have ever visited the island.

Good as new

Sometimes new islands just pop up, seemingly from nowhere. Usually they're the result of a volcanic eruption: lava spews up from an underwater crater, cools and hardens to form a new landmass. Spot one of these and you might get in there first. Just make sure the eruption is well and truly over!

Popping up

New islands that formed in the last 100 years include the following:

Name	Nearest country	Year	Cause	Status
Zalzala Koh	Pakistan	2013	Earthquake	Sinking
Unnamed	Yemen	2012	Undersea volcano	Stable
Home Reef	Tonga	2006	Undersea volcano	Since worn away by waves
Surtsey	Iceland	1963	Undersea volcano	Stable
Ilha Nova	Azores (Portugal)	1957	Undersea volcano	Merged with another island
Anak Krakatau	Indonesia	1927	Undersea volcano	Stable

Make an offer

If your piggy bank is bursting at the seams, perhaps you could buy your own island and declare it a separate state. There are companies that specialize in selling private islands all over the world. For instance, you can pick up a cute little Canadian island with its own forest for about US $40,000. Sure, that's a lot of your allowance, but it's a bargain for what could be the beginning of a great global empire. So start saving!

SOLD

Home away from home

In 1944 a group of Danish schoolteachers bought an island off the coast of Denmark as a place to hold school camps. They declared it the independent Kingdom of Elleore, chose a king, proclaimed laws, and later produced Elleore stamps and coins. Every year, the kingdom's 260 subjects spend one week on the island—they gather to have fun, manage the island's affairs and, when necessary, elect a new monarch. The rest of the time they are said to be "on an extended stay abroad".

UP FOR GRABS

Princess Emily

Scattered around the world are other territories that, for one reason or another, are still unclaimed. Sometimes this is the result of a dispute between nations about where a border should be. In other cases, the lands that are so remote and unappealing that no one wants to live there. Check them out and snap them up!

The Antarctic Pie

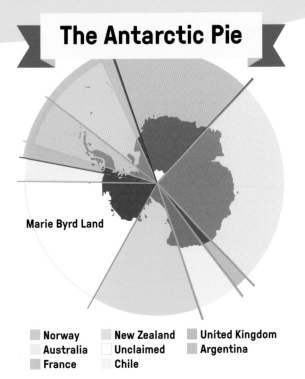

Marie Byrd Land

- Norway
- Australia
- France
- New Zealand
- Unclaimed
- Chile
- United Kingdom
- Argentina

Missing piece

Between 1899 and 1902, British colonial rulers drew two different borders between Egypt and Sudan. As a result, one area, the Hala'ib Triangle, is claimed by both countries, while another, Bir Tawil, is claimed by neither. Sensing an opportunity, American Jeremiah Heaton traveled to Bir Tawil in 2014 to grab it for his daughter, Emily. He named it the Kingdom of North Sudan. But so far no real country has recognized his claim.

Rich pickings

Although it's the world's fifth-largest landmass, Antarctica is also Earth's coldest, driest and windiest environment. Not surprisingly, no one lives there permanently and relatively few people even visit. Though various countries have claimed slices of Antarctica, one large, particularly inhospitable territory remains officially unclaimed: Marie Byrd Land. In addition, the Norwegian sector of Antarctica has no defined southern boundary, so the part near the South Pole could also be up for grabs!

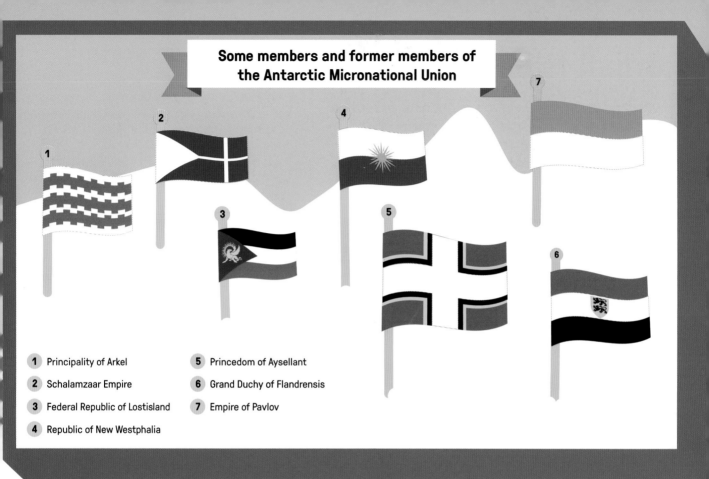

Some members and former members of the Antarctic Micronational Union

1 Principality of Arkel

2 Schalamzaar Empire

3 Federal Republic of Lostisland

4 Republic of New Westphalia

5 Princedom of Aysellant

6 Grand Duchy of Flandrensis

7 Empire of Pavlov

Sorting it out

If you do go for an Antarctic claim, be prepared for serious competition. Talossa claimed most of Marie Byrd Land in 1982, and calls it Pengöpäts. In 2001, American Travis McHenry declared he had founded a country in Marie Byrd Land called the Grand Duchy of Westarctica. And in 2008, a micronation based in Belgium, the Grand Duchy of Flandrensis, claimed five Antarctic islands. In fact so many micronations say they own parts of Antarctica that in 2008 the Antarctic Micronational Union was set up to coordinate their claims. You might want to get in touch.

Loopholes to other worlds

Errors or unclear wording in old laws (known as loopholes) might allow you to proclaim a new country, near home or far away. Stuart Hill, an English resident of the Scottish Shetland Islands, claims the Shetlands were never officially made part of the United Kingdom. In 2008 he therefore declared his tiny home island of Forewick Holm a separate micronation, the Sovereign State of Forvik, and in turn has claimed the rights to any oil found under the island.

Small is beautiful?

With land in short supply, you might have to settle for a teeny territory, some cramped corner of a far-flung continent. Don't despair though: several of the world's most successful real countries are truly and proudly tiny.

Tight fit

Clinging to a steep-sided section of the Mediterranean coastline, Monaco is the world's most densely populated country, with 18,500 people packed into each of its 0.8 sq. miles (2 sq. kilometers). Micro it might be, but Monaco has:

• The world's highest earnings per citizen

• The most millionaires and billionaires of any country

• The world's most expensive houses

• The world's lowest poverty rate

It must be doing something right!

Microstates
These are the world's five smallest countries:
See if you can find them on a map!

1 **Vatican City**
0.17 sq. mi / 0.44 km²

2 **Monaco**
0.78 sq. mi / 2.02 km²

3 **Nauru**
8.1 sq. mi / 21 km²

4 **Tuvalu**
10 sq. mi / 26 km²

5 **San Marino**
24 sq. mi / 61 km²

How big should you go?

Sprawling empire or miniature kingdom? Which way should you go? Consider these two questions and choose the answers that suit you best. Then add your scores to find out how big *your* country should be.

Do you like to get about?
a. You bet: as often as possible and as far afield as I can
b. Yes, but not too far—I'd miss my mom!
c. Now and again, as long as I'm home for dinner.
d. I just stay in my backyard, thanks—can't be too careful.
e. What? I never go out of my room!

Do you like wide, open spaces?
a. Yes! Show me endless plains, limitless horizons, vast skies …
b. Sure, there's nothing better than hiking for miles.
c. Mmm … our local park is *way* big enough for me.
d. You mean I might have to walk?!
e. Are you kidding? *I said* I never go out my room!

a = 5 points   b = 4 points   c = 3 points
d = 2 points   e = 1 point

How did you score?

10 points = XL: There's no limit to what you can manage.

8–9 points = L: Live it large!

6–7 points = M: Not too big, not too small. Steady as she goes!

4–5 points = S: Know your boundaries, right?

2–3 points = XS: Hmm … room state, perhaps?

Who needs land?

Still having trouble finding a foothold? Not to worry.
A lack of land is really no obstacle for an ambitious ruler.
After all, there are other things to put your country on.
Vast expanses of ocean, for example. Or wheels.
Yes, wheels.

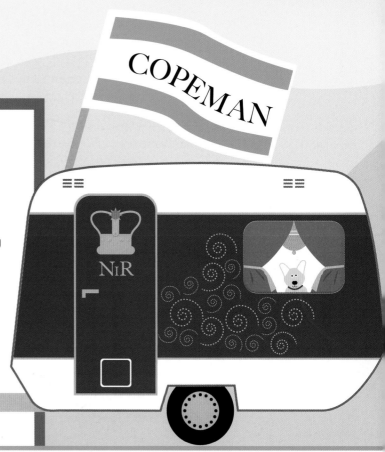

Empire to go

In 2003, 25-year-old Nicholas Copeman decided to become a king. And why not? Then living part-time in a small trailer in Norfolk, England, he declared his mobile home the Copeman Empire, and anointed himself King Nicholas I. Of course, the advantage of having wheels on your empire is that you can take it anywhere, and Nicholas has since enjoyed displaying his realm in different parts of Britain, gaining plenty of attention in the process.

A life on the ocean wave?

The good thing about the sea is that there's plenty of it. Plus, if you go far enough offshore—12 nautical miles (22.2 km)—into international waters, you're beyond the official territory of any nation. But what to live on? A boat could work, but boats can be wobbly, and who wants to be seasick forever? Something more stable would definitely be a better bet.

Blown away

Rafts are easier to build, but they're still fragile. In 1964, Leicester Hemingway, brother of the famous writer Ernest Hemingway, towed a bamboo raft off the coast of Jamaica and proclaimed it the island nation of New Atlantis. He wrote up laws, created a currency, and produced an impressive series of exquisitely designed postage stamps. Unfortunately his country wasn't quite so well made and two years later it was smashed to pieces by a storm.

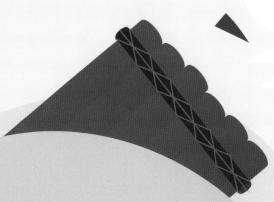

Nation ahoy!

Far more promising than rafts are sea platforms—solid structures anchored to the seabed. These can be tricky to build, but there are some disused ones scattered around the world's oceans. In 1965, former British soldier Roy Bates seized an abandoned military platform off the coast of southeast England, planning to set up a pirate radio station. Two years later, he declared the platform an independent country called the Principality of Sealand. He designed a flag, made up laws, penned a national anthem, and printed passports. Roy died in 2012, but Sealand is still ruled by his son, Prince Michael.

A group called the Seasteading Institute is planning to develop floating cities where people can live together and try out new types of government. These could eventually become new countries!

Worlds beyond

Perhaps nothing suits you here on Earth, or you just like to let your imagination roam much, much further. Maybe you're the kind of person who likes to think outside the box—or even the globe! If so, the possibilities are endless...

The United Federation of Koronis was founded in 2006 by a group of Australians. It claims all territory on eight asteroids between Mars and Jupiter, known as the Koronis group.

Plenty of space

We live on a small planet, in a solar system made up of eight planets, various dwarf planets, many moons, and a Sun, in a tiny corner of a galaxy. Beyond this galaxy are countless others, and measureless space. Somewhere out there, there's got to be a place for you! Others have certainly thought so. Back in 1948, way before the days of moon landings, American James T. Mangan realized that while virtually all the land on Earth was already taken, nobody had claimed outer space. So he registered an official claim and applied to have his vast realm, the Nation of Celestial Space, recognized by the United Nations (UN). And guess what happened? Yes, the UN completely ignored him.

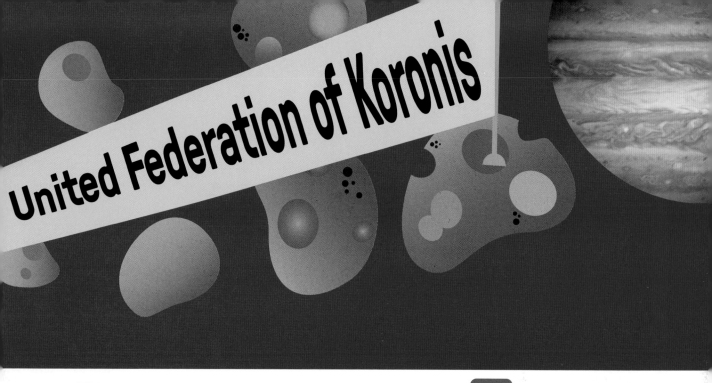

United Federation of Koronis

Virtually yours

In this age of the internet, smartphones and social media, you don't really need land at all. You can set up a country online—a virtual nation where citizens can meet, chat, debate and even do battle, wherever they are. Established in 2008, Wirtland claims to be the world's first online nation. More than 4,000 people have joined it, becoming Witizens of Wirtland, or Wirtlanders. Virtual it might be, but Wirtland has issued real plastic ID cards and metal coins. It even has plans to acquire land and, thereby, just maybe, one day become a real country.

Realms of fantasy

If all else fails, just make it up. Invent another country, map its cities, towns and villages, concoct the life stories and adventures of its inhabitants. It worked for J.R.R. Tolkien, of course. He not only set the *Lord of the Rings* in the fictional world of Middle Earth but also painted illustrations of this realm, drew incredibly detailed maps of its landscapes, invented its languages and even wrote a multi-volume history of its peoples. And to anyone who has spent time there, Middle Earth is far more vivid and real than most of the countries of our world!

Mark your territory

Once you've worked out where your country will be, you need to mark your territory. That might involve drawing lines, building barriers or just putting your country on the map. Read on to find out how.

Shaping up

If your country is your room, your boundaries are clear. If it's in your backyard, it may be at least partly enclosed by your fence or wall. But what if it's somewhere else? How do you mark it out?

Natural boundaries

Of course, if it's an island, the job is already done for you by the sea. Nature can help in other ways, too. Long ago, people accepted obstacles such as rivers and mountain ranges as boundaries between states, and many country borders still follow the shape of such features. For example, the border between France and Spain traces the Pyrenees mountains. In South America, the Paraná and Iguazu rivers separate three nations: Argentina, Brazil and Paraguay. Locals can stand on a riverbank and wave to people in two other countries. Cool, huh? Are there natural features that mark the edge of your country?

Triple Frontier

A Brazil **B** Argentina **C** Paraguay

Drawing lines

What if your country is in the middle of open land? How do you create its borders? Just get out the paint and slap down a rough line? Not exactly. Countries normally employ people called surveyors to establish where borders are on land. They use various instruments and mathematical calculations to work out distances and angles and then plot the lines on a map. Usually the lines are then marked on the ground with posts or pillars. If your country isn't huge, you could use a long piece of string and some wooden pegs or stakes to mark out its boundaries.

On the ground

Some borders are drawn only on paper and entirely invisible on land. No one is quite sure, for example, where the borders between the United Arab Emirates (a small state in the Middle East) and its neighbors, Saudi Arabia and Oman, really lie. But given that the area is barren desert, no one much cares either. Other boundaries are more … well … clear-cut. Much of the dividing line between Norway and Sweden, for example, is a long, narrow clearing through dense forest—in other words, a huge green stripe. There's an idea: maybe you can mark your border with a mower!

Where am I?

More than 6,000 stone pillars mark the border between India and Nepal. In 2014 it was discovered that more than 1,400 of these pillars were missing—in an area notorious for smuggling. Border guards had to use maps to try to work out where the line they were supposed to be protecting actually was!

BORDER SECURITY

Is a mark on the ground or a line of posts enough, or do you need something a bit more substantial? A fence? A wall? Guard posts manned by fierce-looking sentries? Moats filled with sharks? Better think it through carefully.

Who goes there?

Even where there's no need for a continuous physical boundary around your country, it's usually a good idea to have checkpoints where people are most likely to come and go. A checkpoint can be a simple barrier, or a gate where people have to stop and ask permission to enter.

Opting out

In 1982, the setting up of a border checkpoint failed big time for the United States. In an attempt to halt drug smuggling from the Caribbean, government authorities in Florida placed a passport checkpoint across the bridge that divides the city of Key West and other island settlements from the Florida mainland. The islands' residents were so annoyed by this obstruction, which interfered with business and tourism, that they decided to declare themselves an independent state, the Conch Republic. Despite failing to receive official recognition, it now has a government office, a flag and a website. It even issues passports!

Assessing the threats

Answer the following questions to find out what level of protection your country requires.

Who are your neighbors?
1. Just the occasional puzzled onlooker, and one or two cows.
2. A few nice families.
3. My annoying brother/sister/neighbor's kids.
4. Lots of people I don't even know.

Have you had disagreements with them in the past?
1. No, I get on well with everyone.
2. Hmm, I have upset a few neighbors.
3. Yes, and now they're always trying to get the better of me.
4. I'm convinced they're out to sabotage my country!

Do they look friendly?
1. Yes, somebody even waved.
2. One or two smile, but some look a bit stern.
3. Sort of, but I don't trust them.
4. No, and I've been getting some really dirty looks.

How did you score?

Add up the numbers of your answers, so if you picked option 1, score one point, and so on. Design your borders according to your total score:

3–4: No one's likely to bother you. Have a few "Welcome!" signs at strategic points.

5–8: Might be good to take some precautions: put up some "Private Property'" or "No Entry!" signs.

9–10: Best have a fence. Place checkpoints on all possible access routes. Search people.

11–12: Start building a wall, and build it tall. Get a big dog.

Not welcome

If you sense there's always going to be trouble, a big, high barrier may be the only way to go. And it will certainly send a clear message. Claiming it was threatened by terrorists, Israel began building a giant "separation barrier," up to 26ft. (8m) high, along its border with the Palestinian West Bank territory in 2002. When completed it will be 430mi (700km) long. And in an effort to stop Mexican people sneaking into its country without passports, the United States has built several high fences topped with barbed wire along sections of its southern frontier. One even divides the beach at Tijuana.

Welcome to Panmunjom

Bordering on the ridiculous

Sometimes nations agree to leave a gap between their countries. This is called a "buffer zone," or "no-man's-land." Founded in 1992 by two Swedish artists, the micronation known as the Kingdoms of Elgaland-Vargaland has claimed as its territory all international borderlines (as they supposedly belong to no one), all buffer zones and all other gaps between countries. The kingdom's rulers claim this makes it the world's only global nation!

A table divided

After fighting a war from 1950 to 1953, the countries of North Korea and South Korea remain sworn enemies. Along the border between them they have constructed a buffer zone 160mi (260km) long and 2.5mi (4km) wide. It is called the Demilitarized Zone (DMZ), even though it is guarded by two million troops to stop people from crossing the zone. But to permit negotiators to talk, without leaving their countries, the borderline runs through the middle of a long table in a conference room at Panmunjom.

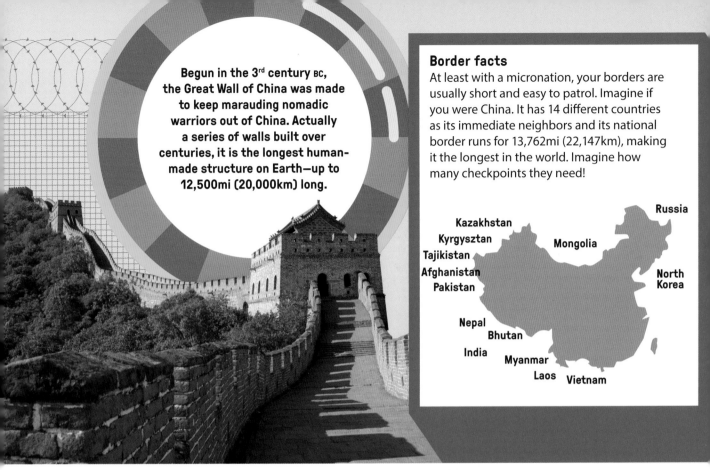

Begun in the 3rd century BC, the Great Wall of China was made to keep marauding nomadic warriors out of China. Actually a series of walls built over centuries, it is the longest human-made structure on Earth—up to 12,500mi (20,000km) long.

Border facts

At least with a micronation, your borders are usually short and easy to patrol. Imagine if you were China. It has 14 different countries as its immediate neighbors and its national border runs for 13,762mi (22,147km), making it the longest in the world. Imagine how many checkpoints they need!

Russia
Kazakhstan
Kyrgysztan
Tajikistan
Mongolia
Afghanistan
Pakistan
North Korea
Nepal
Bhutan
India
Myanmar
Laos
Vietnam

Countries within countries

If your sister claims her old desk in the middle of your room state and you let her have it, that desk becomes what's called an "enclave"—a piece of territory inside one country that belongs to another. Enclaves are sometimes left behind when borders are redrawn. Perhaps the most bizarre is Dahala Khagrabari, near the India-Bangladesh border. It's a parcel of Indian land that is inside a Bangladeshi village that is encircled by an Indian village that is in turn surrounded by Bangladesh. In other words, it's an enclave of an enclave of an enclave. Got it?

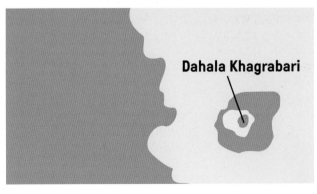

Dahala Khagrabari

■ India   ■ Bangladesh

Looks good on paper

Once you've worked out the precise shape of your country, it's a good idea to create a map. Then you can give your map to friends, neighbors and other rulers so that they can see exactly where and how big your country is.

Measure up

To make a map, you need to know the position and size of your country. Use a compass to work out where north is. If your country is a small area, like part of your backyard, you may be able to measure it (and some of its features) with a tape measure. (Alternatively, work out how many of your paces make 100 feet and then measure the approximate distance by walking it.) If, on the other hand, you've claimed a distant territory, you'll need to find a good map of it and look at the scale. On most maps this is shown as a bar, like this:

On the grid

A great way to draw a map is by using a grid. Grab a ruler and pencil and mark ten even spaces (say of 1in each) across the top and bottom of a page and ten down on each side. Join the marks with your ruler to create a grid. If your backyard state is 800ft. long and 400ft. wide, you can draw it eight squares long and four wide, with each square representing 100ft. Or if your distant territory is 20mi long and 10mi wide, you can draw it as ten squares by five, with each square representing 2mi. Got it? Below is an example on a smaller scale.

0   40mi

In this case, 1 inch equals 10 miles. So if the territory is 2 inches on the map, it's actually 20 miles long.

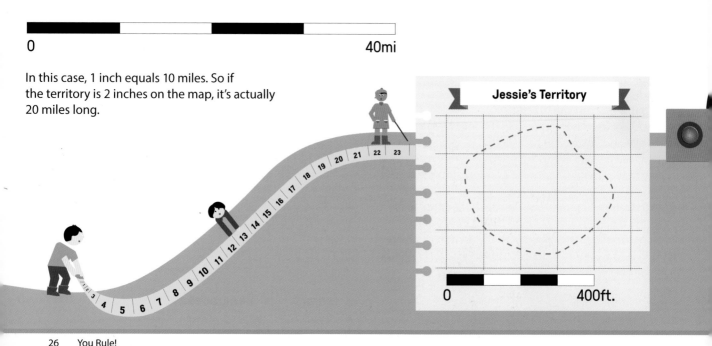

Jessie's Territory

0   400ft.

Color coding

Draw your country's border clearly with a single thick line—red always looks official. Then draw other major features of your country, in the correct positions and, as far as possible, at the right scale. Normally, maps show different kinds of natural or physical features with different colors; deserts are brown or pale yellow, grasslands are yellow or pale green, forests are dark green, waterways are blue, paths may be dashed lines. On simple maps, mountain peaks or hilltops can be drawn as a line of peaks or marked with a triangle. Get out your color pencils and code the physical features of your country, and include a key to explain each colour. You can add other features to the map as your country develops.

Maps are usually (but not always) drawn so that north is at the top. Add an arrow or a compass symbol (known as a compass rose) to your map to show which way is north.

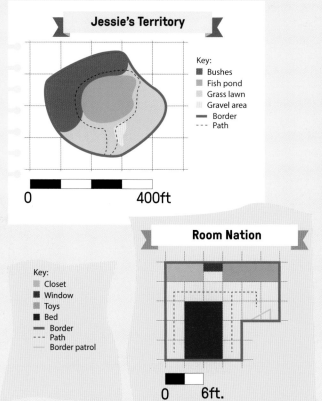

Jessie's Territory

Key:
- Bushes
- Fish pond
- Grass lawn
- Gravel area
- — Border
- --- Path

0   400ft

Room Nation

Key:
- Closet
- Window
- Toys
- Bed
- — Border
- --- Path
- Border patrol

0   6ft.

Persistence pays

It's hard work getting your country onto official maps. Normally you have to prove that it and its boundaries have been recognized by other, proper nations. But persistence can pay. The micronation known as the Principality of Hutt River was founded by Leonard Casley in 1970, on a wheat farm north of Perth, Australia, after he had a dispute with the Australian government about wheat prices. It has since become so well known as a tourist attraction that it now appears on Google Maps. Look it up!

PRINCIPALITY OF HUTT RIVER

3 Make it official

So now you have a territory and you know exactly where it is. But does anyone else? You need to spread the word! Declare the birth of a nation, raise a flag and celebrate your country's glorious foundation!

What's in a name?

Hang on, though, what's your country called? You have got a name for it, haven't you? What do you mean, "still thinking about it?" Never mind, help is at hand.

Short but sweet

Is there an idea behind your country, or is it just about you? If you're determined to grab all the glory for yourself, go ahead. It's your country, after all.

If you're feeling lazy, you could just add "-land" to your name: "Emmaland," "Tomland," or "Kimland," for instance. Or, if you prefer not to be the focus of attention, you could use a simple descriptive name, like "Longland," or "Forestland." It worked for Iceland after all! But perhaps you do have a theme for your country—be it noble, romantic or just plain daft—such as harmony, happiness, music or fish. Fishland? Hmm, maybe not ...

GREENLAND

Did you know? Viking explorer Erik the Red came up with the name "Greenland" in the hope of attracting settlers to the icy realm.

Happy endings

To jazz up a simple one-word name, try some other suffixes (bits you add to the end of words). Just a couple of letters, for example, turn Kimland into something more glamorous: "Kimlandia." Nice, huh? You could give it an exotic feel with "-stan," which means "land" in various languages: "Kimistan." Whatever you choose, it has to sound just right.

Finishing touch

For a final dash of grandeur and glamour, try an adjective (or two) at the front. Make your country "Grand" or "Great," "Immortal," or "Most Noble." The famous and historic microstate in Italy known as San Marino isn't really just San Marino, you know. Officially, it's the Most Serene Republic of San Marino. Doesn't that sound wonderful?

Most Serene Republic of
San Marino

Royal ring

Just using a single word might be seen as a bit lacking in ambition, which is the last thing you want! Using two or three words—the *something* of Kimlandia—immediately gives a country name a grander air. And to most budding rulers, it's all the more pleasing if it has a royal ring to it. So why not make your country sound really grand by calling it a principality, a kingdom, or even an empire. "The Empire of Kimistan"—now you're talking!

Your choice of state name might depend on what title you fancy as ruler. Which sounds right for you?

Type of State	Head of State
Empire	Emperor or Empress
Kingdom	King or Queen
Principality	Prince or Princess
Duchy	Duke or Duchess
Republic	President
Federation	President or King/Queen

The name game

If you're still stuck, this handy table should help you out. Just pick a name, then add other words in the order shown below. If you really can't decide (which, let's face it, isn't a good start for the ruler of a new country), simply roll a die three times to select one name from each category.

So, for example, if you roll 4, 3 and 2 and your name is Tom, your country is the "Most Noble Principality of Tomlandia." Not bad!

1. Grand	Empire	of NAME	-land
2. Great	Kingdom	of NAME	-landia
3. Immortal	Principality	of NAME	-istan
4. Most Noble	Duchy	of NAME	-ania
5. Sovereign	Federation	of NAME	-topia
6. United	Republic	of NAME	-ica

Ready to fly

After a country name, the next essential thing for any new ruler is a flag. You'll need one for ceremonies, for claiming new territories, for rallying your troops and for your citizens to stick on their car bumpers.

Nailing your colors

It's fairly easy to design your own flag. Most consist of simple blocks of color, so it makes sense to start there. Perhaps you could use your favorite color, or something that you feel represents your country: blue for an island in a vast sea, green for land cloaked with forests or purple for the color of the walls in your room!

Building blocks

Play around with blocks of different colors. You could opt for a two-color, flag like Ukraine's plain blue and yellow design. Or the very popular tricolor (three colors) style favored by the likes of France and Italy. Just make sure it hasn't been done before. Clearly, Indonesia and Monaco didn't do their homework on this and both have ended up with the same flag—a white block below a red block. And Poland's flag is the same but upside down. Come on guys, make an effort!

From 1977 to 2011, Libya had the world's only flag of just one color, a plain green rectangle. Talk about keeping things simple!

Okay, so which is Monaco? See, hopeless!

Outside the box

For a bit more style and variety, get away from simple squares or rectangles and add a few curves and angles. You could throw in a circle, try some stripes or a cross, maybe even a star or two (or 50 if you want to copy the United States), or why not have your lines run diagonally, in all sorts of colors, like the Seychelles? Now does that not just say "fun place" to you?!

Pole position

You can make your flag more distinctive by adding a symbol that represents your country. It could be a strong and powerful looking animal—Albania's flag has a two-headed black eagle, and Bhutan's has a seriously cool-looking dragon. Or how about a symbol that relates to the landscapes of your country, like Canada's maple leaf, or something that refers to your nation's theme? Beaming out from the flag of the Aerican Empire, a micronation devoted to silliness, is a huge smiley face.

It's a wrap!

Once you are happy with your design, paint a giant version on to thick paper or card, or ask an adult to help you sew a real one out of different color fabrics. Then attach it to a pole and get ready to fly it!

Simple is best

Remember it's best to keep it simple: choose a pattern you can confidently draw and print, and that your subjects can easily copy for their own homemade flags, which they'll wave at you when you pass by.

The scientific study of flags is called "vexillology" and an expert on flags is called a "vexillologist." A designer of flags is a "vexillographer" and if you are someone who likes flags you can call yourself a "vexillophile." As long as you can get your tongue round it!

Herald a new nation

While you've got your pencils and paints out and your artistic thinking cap on, it's a good idea to design a coat of arms, too. These fancy symbols are pretty snazzy and will give your banners, letters and proclamations a seriously official look.

YOU RULE!

Badge of honour

Emblems and symbols were used by ancient empires, but it was in the Middle Ages that they became all the rage. Every wealthy family, city, and state wanted its own stylish symbol, and strict rules for designing them were written down and are still used today. The study of such symbols is called "heraldry" and the symbols are known as "heraldic symbols." Most real countries have at least one, and yours should be no exception.

Quite an achievement

Known also as an achievement, a heraldic symbol is usually made up of the same bits and pieces. At the centre is a shield with patterns or images on it: the coat of arms. On either side of the shield are animals that look like they're holding it up: the supporters. Above the shield is a helmet (helm) with a fancy top (crest) and below is a banner bearing a motto, or short saying.

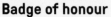

Carve it out

Design yourself a heraldic symbol, including images that relate to your country. Start with the coat of arms. It can be divided into colored panels, or have a picture on it. What might your supporters be? Scary-looking lions? Unicorns? Your pet guinea pigs? Draw it on paper first. If you're a bit handy, you could make one out of balsa wood or polystyrene, paint it and hang it in your throne room.

Secret messages

Some symbols can be a bit mysterious. Argentina's coat of arms shows what looks like a red beanie hat stuck on the end of a pole. To those in the know, however, the hat is a traditional symbol of freedom.

I say!

A motto is meant to sum up the ideals of your country. Traditionally, mottoes were in Latin, but if your Latin is a bit rusty or you think none of your subjects will understand, stick with English. A motto could be something like "Happy together," or "With honesty and decency." Greece has "Freedom or death," which at least gives Greeks a simple choice! The African country of Botswana, a parched land where a downpour is always welcomed, favors just one hopeful word, *pula*, meaning "rain."

Micro mottoes

These micronation mottoes might give you some ideas:

A light in the darkness
Empire of Atlantium

A man's room is his kingdom
Kingdom of Talossa

While I breathe, I hope
Principality of Hutt River

From the sea, freedom
Principality of Sealand

Nothing ventured, nothing gained
Republic of Molossia

With laws the land will be built
Sovereign State of Forvik

To secede means to separate from another country, or become independent. The motto of the Conch Republic is "We seceded where others failed." Ha!

Declare yourself!

Now you've got a name, a flag and official symbols, it's time to proclaim your nation's existence. Make sure everyone knows what, who and where you are. Then bring together as many people as you can to mark your country's beginnings—and prepare for a magnificent future!

Get the word out

Let everyone know your nation is open and ready for business. Call or email all your friends. Put up posters, hand out leaflets, and drop flyers in your neighbors' letterboxes. Tell them about your country and ask them to drop by.

Have a foundation day

Organize a ceremony to mark the foundation of your country. Invite your family, friends, and neighbors. Then work out what you're actually going to do! People are much more likely to come if you lay on some live music and tasty food. At the very least, raise a flag. With everyone watching, plant it firmly on a prominent part of your territory. It will look especially impressive if you can get hold of a proper flagpole.

Flag-raising rules

Check your flag is clean and not damaged or faded. Select people in advance for special roles in your ceremony and proceed as follows:

- Group of officials (the color guard) carry in the flag

- Another official (color bearer) accepts the flag and unfolds it (making sure it doesn't touch the ground)

- Color bearer attaches flag to the flag pole (checking it's not upside down)

- Flagpole is planted or hoisted, briskly and with dignity

- Everyone looks up at the flag, in awe.

Words up

To make your ceremony especially memorable, read out a declaration of independence. This is a document that announces that you have created a separate, independent state. Many countries began with documents like this, most famously the United States, whose Declaration of Independence was finalized and proclaimed in 1776, on 4 July—now U.S. Independence Day.

Write stuff

Keep your declaration fairly short—you don't want listeners nodding off or suddenly remembering they have other appointments. Make sure it includes the following:

- The name of your new country and its location

- The country from which you are separating (seceding)

- Why you are doing it

- What you hope to achieve.

Point the way

It's vital that you get people excited about your new country. So make sure you explain what you plan to do and why it will be truly magnificent. What are your goals? Just to have fun? The creation of an adult-free zone? World domination? Make sure people know and are inspired.

Make it forever

Remember this is a day that will go down in history (well, yours at least), so make sure you have someone take lots of photographs or video.

Making the grade

It's the goal of every new nation to gain official recognition, to be treated by other, established countries as an equal. Achieving that, however, is no mean feat. In fact, it's so tricky that no micronation has yet managed it. But, hey, you like a challenge, right?

By the rules

So how do you get to be a real country? What makes a nation? A famous treaty signed in 1933 in South America, the *Montevideo Convention on the Rights and Duties of States*, set out the following four requirements: a defined territory, a permanent population, a government, and an ability to enter into relations with other countries.

How are you shaping up?

Take the Montevideo test to find out if your country has got what it takes.

Breaking away

Even if you meet the requirements of the Montevideo Convention, there's still a major stumbling block. To be accepted as a real country, you need other countries to officially recognize you. So start making friends with your nearest neighbors. Write to whoever previously held your territory and tell them you're taking it over. Ask them to recognize your new state. If they're not happy about it, they'll let you know. If they don't respond, you can assume either they aren't willing to recognize your country or, looking on the bright side, they really don't mind!

1. Defined Territory?
You should have worked this out by now. Even if it is just your room.

2. Permanent population
At the very least, there's you. Friends and family too, right? You're on your way!

3. Government
It's still on the to-do list, but you'll get there soon (at least by page 55)

4. Relationships with other countries
Well, you're friendly and outgoing and ready for fun, aren't you? So that's sorted then. Looks like you're on track!

World stage

If you crave certainty and a global profile, the next step is to apply for membership of the United Nations. Based in New York, this is an organization to which almost all the world's real countries belong. It is a place where their representatives can hang out, discuss problems and agree on solutions, and it's the closest thing we have to a world government. Gain membership here and you're made! The trouble is, they're a bit fussy about who they let in. Even some real countries haven't been accepted.

How to apply for UN membership

1. Declare your country a "peace-loving state."

2. Write an application saying you accept all the rules of the UN and would love to join.

3. Gain the approval of at least nine of the UN's 15 Council members, and the approval of all five permanent members—China, France, Russia, the United Kingdom and the United States.

4. Have your application approved by a vote of all UN members—you need at least two-thirds to say yes.

5. Pay your annual fees.

With your powers of persuasion, it'll be a breeze!

☑ CHINA
☐ FRANCE
☐ RUSSIA
☐ UK
☐ USA

Moments of glory

On 5 June 1958, James T. Mangan, founder of the Nation of Celestial Space (see page 18) unveiled his nation's flag on a U.S. TV show. It was a hash sign—a traditional printer's sign for space—on a blue background. Millions were watching the show, so it was a brilliant way to gain widespread recognition. Even better, the next day he managed to persuade someone at the UN headquarters in New York to raise his flag alongside those of its member nations. Though it took only a day for the organization to realize its mistake and pull the flag down, it was a stunning triumph for a budding nation.

Bring a crowd

It's not going to be much of a country if it doesn't have any people. So involve your family, invite more friends and neighbors. If it's a cool place to be, word will soon spread and plenty more people will start turning up. Give it a few generations and you could have a proper population.

Come visit!

Try to find more ways to attract people to your country. Get yourself noticed and get people interested. Persuade them your country is a great place to go.

Press ahead

Contact your local newspaper and let them know what you are up to. Write to other newspapers and local radio stations too. Tell them you are holding a press conference to announce the creation of your new nation and invite them to send reporters and photographers to interview you. You always wanted to get your picture in the papers, didn't you?

Happening place

Add a news page to your website, if you have one, so that people can find out what's happening in your country. Social media sites are a great way to spread the news of your nation's glorious birth, too. Make your country sound like a happening place—even if it does only exist online!

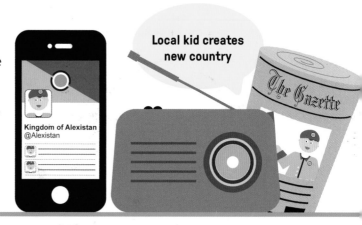

Kingdom of Alexistan
@Alexistan

Local kid creates new country

The Gazette

Show your colors

You can increase awareness of your country in other ways too. Print flags and signs on paper and ask if you can pin them up in public places like libraries and tourism offices—it will make people eager to find out more. Have some stylish badges and tee shirts made and ask friends to wear them.

In the picture

Try photobombing: when you see someone taking a picture, walk behind them wearing your tee shirt or carrying a flag, so that they take a picture of you and your national colors too. Soon your flag will be popping up in photo albums all over the world!

Join the jet set

Take some pictures of your country—only the nicest parts of course—and write some short articles about its attractions. Could your country be a fashionable new vacation destination? Use the pictures and stories to make a brochure about your country. Give it to family and friends. Ask your teachers if you can hand it out at school, or leave it at reception in the entrance hall to get more interest from your classmates and visitors.

Permanent vacation

In 1952, while travelling in Israel, Eli Aviv came across an abandoned property on the country's border with the Lebanon. He took it over and declared it the State of Akhzivland, and even managed to halt Israeli government attempts to reclaim the territory. Akhzivland just happened to be on a beautiful stretch of coastline, and to this day Aviv attracts a small but steady flow of tourists to stay in his beachside state, where he happily welcomes visitors and stamps their passports.

Stay Forever!

Once people start visiting, you might find they want to stay longer, even permanently. Don't worry if you haven't got room for them all, you can still invite them to become part of your population—citizens of your new nation.

INCOMING **OUTGOING**

Where do they go?
Among the 230 million people who have moved to another country, these are the five most popular destinations:

United States	45 million
Russian Federation	11 million
Germany	9.8 million
Saudi Arabia	9.1 million
United Arab Emirates	7.8 million

Where do they come from?
These are the top five countries of origin of the world's 230 million migrants:

India	14 million
Mexico	13 million
Russian Federation	10.8 million
China	9.3 million
Bangladesh	7.8 million

On the move
Many people are eager to move to a different country, or migrate, in the hope of finding a better life or just experiencing a different culture. And some people, sadly, have to flee their own countries as a result of violence or persecution and seek refuge somewhere else. Today, more than 230 million people are living in a different country from the one they were born in. People are always on the move and nice new countries are always of interest.

No room

So, if your country is appealing, you could have people queuing up at your door. Just make sure you are clear about what you are offering. In 1980, artist Lars Vilks built two huge sculptures on a remote beach in southern Sweden. He declared the virtually uninhabited 0.4 sq. mi (1 sq. km) area an independent nation, called Ladonia. Later, when Vilks started offering citizenship applications on his website, more than 4,000 people from Pakistan applied to live in his country! Vilks had to point out that there wasn't actually room for them there—oops! Still, 17,000 people have become Ladonian citizens and more than 40,000 tourists visit each year.

In 2005, British TV comedian Danny Wallace persuaded 55,000 people to become citizens of a country he had set up in his room in London, called Lovely.

Like-minded

Think about the kind of people you want to have as citizens of your country. Do they need to share your ideas and beliefs? In Denmark in 1971, a group of people eager to live a different lifestyle took over an old military camp and proclaimed it a micronation, the Freetown of Christiania. They agreed to live without cars and police, drew up their own laws and created their own currency, the Løn. Today Christiania is home to about 1,000 people, visited by more than 70,000 tourists a year and famous for its three-wheeled "Christiania bicycles."

Life Members

So what can you offer your citizens? A place to hang out, or just a country to be part of from afar? How will they benefit by being citizens and what will they enjoy about your country? And exactly what do you want them to give you in return?

It's a deal!

A good way to set things straight is to have people sign or swear an oath of citizenship. This sets out what you are offering and what you expect of your citizens. It goes without saying that they should first offer eternal devotion and undying loyalty to you. You might also ask them to swear allegiance to your flag, help you improve the country, and be prepared to sacrifice their lives to defend your nation in the event of war. That's not too much to ask, is it? In return, you will give them a fancy certificate of citizenship and the opportunity to be part of a fun and no doubt all-round awesome nation.

KINGDOM OF ALEXISTAN

Certificate of
Citizenship

Awarded to: **Mom**

Authorized by our Great Leader

Swearing in

Start with your family and friends. Have them attend an official ceremony, where they read out the oath of loyalty and are presented with their citizenship certificate.

Doubling up

Until your country realizes its full, glorious potential, some citizens might just prefer to keep their options open. So make sure you offer dual nationality. This means that people can become citizens of your country while remaining citizens of another. Twice the fun!

National ID

There's another thing you can offer that will not only be treasured by your citizens, but also gain nods of approval from other nations: a passport. A passport is a document stating that the holder is a citizen of a nation and thereby has the freedom to come and go from that country and enter other countries. Issuing passports is a hallmark of a *serious* nation.

How to make a passport

Most passports take the form of a booklet containing the holder's personal information and blank pages for other countries to fill with fancy stamps. Here's how to make your own:

1. Cut out three or four sheets of pale-colored paper 7in (18cm) wide and 5in (12.5cm) tall. Cut out a sheet of darker-colored card of the same size. Line up the card and paper, fold it in half to create a booklet and staple together along the spine.

2. On the cover, print the official name of your country and draw your national coat of arms or flag. For a stylish and seriously official look, use gold or silver ink.

3. On the inside front cover or first page, include this declaration: *'I, [your title as ruler], leader of [name of country], request all those whom it may concern to allow the bearer of this document to pass freely without hindrance, and to offer any assistance he or she may require.'* Add your signature underneath.

4. On the second page or last page, place a square outline where the holder can paste their photograph, and a form for them to fill in:

Name	Sex M/F (male or female)
Date of birth	Date of issue
Place of birth	Date of expiry
Nationality	Signature

5. Give each passport a different number.

That should look the part (though it's not going to fool any real customs officers!).

Visiting citizens

Nami Island is a popular tourist destination on South Korea's Han River. In 2006, it declared itself the independent Naminara Republic, a "fairy-tale country" on "an island of songs." To visit, you have to first buy a visa; or for an extra payment, you can purchase a one-year passport. About 1.5 million tourists visit every year and many opt for the passport. That's one way to boost your population!

Settling in

With a little nurturing, your people will prosper and your population will grow. But if your citizens are coming to stay, you need to make sure you have plenty of room for them—and know how to manage a crowd.

Caught in the rush

If a country looks like fun, its population can grow rapidly as more and more people want to join in. It'll grow even faster if those people settle there and have children. After industries boomed in the United States in the mid-1800s, more than 30 million people migrated there between 1870 and 1930, and the population leapt from 38 million to 123 million!

Micro pops

Of course, with a micronation, you'll probably keep things small scale. Some rulers want a nation all to themselves, or are happy with one or two friends or even just a pet for company. President Kevin Baugh founded his Republic of Molossia at his home in Dayton, Nevada, USA, in 1999. Despite gaining worldwide attention, he refuses applications for citizenship from outsiders and limits his population to his family—initially just three immediate family members, but now 21 relatives and six dogs.

Head counts

Today China has the world's biggest population. But India's is growing faster, and India may overtake China as the world's most populous nation by 2030.

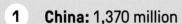

Top five most populous countries

1	**China:**	1,370 million
2	**India:**	1,260 million
3	**USA:**	319 million
4	**Indonesia:**	252 million
5	**Brazil:**	203 million

WELCOME new citizens!

Doing the numbers

Are you a people person? Take this test to find out how many people you should invite to your country.

It's sunny outside and you have a free afternoon. What do you do?
1. Read at home, with the drapes shut.
2. Ask a friend to go for a wilderness hike.
3. Invite all your neighbors for a barbecue.
4. Hit the shopping mall, go see a movie then attend a huge sporting event.

A friend asks you to a big party. How do you respond?
1. Say, "No thanks, I'm going to wash my hair."
2. Feel terrified but go, then speak to no one.
3. Go along with a few friends and have a fine old time.
4. Arrive alone, talk to everyone and leave having made heaps of new BFFs.

You're asked to raise money for charity. How do you approach it?
1. Do a solo sponsored hike but don't tell anyone and pay the money yourself.
2. Coordinate a bake sale at your school with a couple of classmates.
3. Organize a group of family and friends to collect money around the neighborhood.
4. Set up a planning committee, involve your whole town, obtain national TV coverage and form an international network of big-business sponsors.

How did you score?

Add up the numbers of your answers to find your ideal population size:

3–4
Keep to single figures. Make it online only. You don't want to overdo things.

5–6
Hundreds maybe, but mostly online. Invite a select few to visit, but don't let them stay.

7–9
Thousands. Ask the ones with most to offer to move in and help you out.

10–12
The sky's the limit. Encourage settlement, get people working for you. Look forward to putting your feet up.

Getting cozy

Watch out! If your country is on the compact side, it could quickly become very crowded. Some parts of the world have become so popular that millions of people live crammed together in a small area. And they include some of the world's smallest countries. Let that be a lesson to you!

Top five most densely populated countries

Country	People per sq. mile	People per sq. km
Monaco	47,850	18,475
Singapore	19,731	7,618
Vatican City	4,709	1,818
Bahrain	4,224	1,631
Malta	3,421	1,321

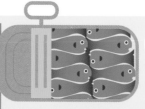

Talk about cozy!

Capital choice
Even in more spacious countries people tend to gather in particular places, or settlements—called villages, towns and cities, depending on their size. Before that happens, make sure you get in first and claim the best spot for your nation's capital. That's where you'll have your official government buildings and, ideally, your magnificent royal palace (though you might have to settle for a cozy garden shed or a cool tree house).

Room to roam
A big territory will of course allow you to spread your citizens out. This has its advantages, as people like open spaces for relaxing, wandering around, and walking their dogs. Then again, if it's too big, people might feel a bit lonely. In parts of Australia, for example, farms are separated by enormous distances. One cattle farm called Anna Creek, in South Australia, covers 9,142 sq. mi (23,677 sq. km), making it larger than many real countries!

Hey! Where'd everybody go?!

Top five least densely populated countries

Country	People per sq. mile	People per sq. km
Mongolia	4.56	1.76
Namibia	6.63	2.56
Australia	7.98	3.08
Iceland	8.16	3.15
Suriname	8.44	3.26

Popping up

Most of your citizens will want to live near you, naturally, and the capital will probably become your country's major centre. But if your population grows, people may spread to other places, and settlements could pop up everywhere. Remember to update your country map every so often, to keep track of new places and features.

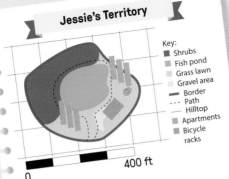

Jessie's Territory

Key:
- Shrubs
- Fish pond
- Grass lawn
- Gravel area
- Border
- Path
- Hilltop
- Apartments
- Bicycle racks

0   400 ft

Water way

You might not think you have room for cities, but they can sprout in the oddest places. Who'd think that a cluster of small, muddy islands would be a good place to live? But that's where the city of Venice developed off the northeast coast of Italy in the 6th century. Quickly running out of land, the citizens began to use waterways as streets—as they do to this day.

High rise

Sometimes cities get so crowded that the only way is up. High-rise apartment buildings can house huge numbers of people. In the 1980s, one cluster of high-rise buildings in the tiny territory of Hong Kong, which measured little more than 328ft. by 656ft. (100m by 200m), was home to 35,000 people. That's the equivalent of 3.24 million per sq mi (1.25 million people per sq km)!

Today Hong Kong has by far the highest number of high-rises of any place in the world, with over 300 buildings standing more than 500ft (150m) tall.

Show who's boss

Who's in charge here? You, of course. But you have to decide what kind of leader you want to be. Are you going it alone or will you get some help? If your country gets bigger, you might need to let your people make their own decisions. It's hard to let go, isn't it? But it's the sign of a grown-up nation.

Going solo

Leaders that like to go it alone, keeping sole control of everything, are known as autocrats, and their countries are called autocracies.

God-like powers
In ancient times, autocrats often claimed they had been appointed by a god or were gods themselves. Several Egyptian rulers, for example, claimed to be earthly forms of the gods Amun and Ra. Alexander the Great, of Macedonia, liked to say he had been fathered by Zeus, greatest of the Greek gods. This sort of thing seemed to work a treat then, but you may have trouble convincing your subjects today.

Losing the plot
Being an autocrat is all very well if your country stays tiny. But if it starts to grow, autocracy could be a recipe for disaster. It will be almost impossible to manage everything by yourself. You're likely to get exhausted, and probably a bit grumpy. And if that happens, you could even start behaving like a tyrant—ordering people around, ticking them off constantly, and much, much worse!

Terrible tyrants

Once you become a tyrant, your reputation as a leader will be in tatters. And if you really go power-crazy, you could end up like these guys—some of the most feared and loathed leaders in history.

Qin Shihuang

The First Emperor of China (246–210 BC) had almost anyone who disagreed with him killed. He also forced 700,000 people to work on his gigantic tomb, which included a vast underground palace, and had many of the builders, along with his own wives, buried alive inside the tomb when he died.

Nero

Roman emperor from AD 54–68, Nero had no qualms about executing opponents, even his mother. When much of Rome was burned in a fire, he blamed it on the Christians, some of whom he personally punished by dipping them in oil, setting them on fire and using them as nightlights in his backyard.

Genghis Khan

Leader of the mighty Mongol Empire from 1206–27, Genghis liked nothing better than raiding and destroying cities, and his armies slaughtered millions in Central Asia. Genghis kept count by collecting the ears of his victims.

Vlad the Impaler

Prince of Wallachia (in modern-day Hungary) from 1431–76, Vlad gained a fearful reputation for cruelty across Europe, partly as a result of his liking for impaling enemies on pointed sticks. Ouch! He is said to have helped inspire the legend of Dracula the vampire.

Ivan the Terrible

You don't get a nickname like that by being nice. Increasingly unable to control his temper, Ivan, czar of Russia from 1547–84, famously beat his own son to death. Suspecting the people of Novgorod of treason, in 1570 he had up to 12,000 of them tortured as he watched. Charming!

Tyrant: from the Greek *tyrannos*, meaning a strict, oppressive leader.

Power sharing

One way to spread the load is to involve your family. Declare a monarchy and call yourself king or queen, then your little brother can be a prince and your sister a princess. They'll love that! And if it's what's called a "hereditary monarchy," any children you have will rule after you—and then their children, and so on.

Keeping it in the family
The world's longest-lasting monarchy is the Imperial House of Japan, which began in 660 BC. That means one family has ruled Japan for almost 2,700 years. Nice work!

PET POWER

Could your pets get involved? It has happened. After the township of Whangamomona in New Zealand declared itself an independent republic in 1989 it elected, as its second president, a goat called Billy Gumboot (also known as Billy the Kid). He was succeeded by a poodle, called Tai.

Chosen ones
Need more help? Organize your government like a private club. Invite some friends to take charge of important jobs, such as keeping track of your riches, writing proclamations and organizing lavish parties. Make decisions together and share the spoils. This style of government is known as an "oligarchy." Sounds a bit selfish, though, doesn't it? And it's not likely to go down well with your subjects.

BILLY

Let them have it

A fairer option is to involve every one of your citizens in government. This is known as "democracy" and it was first introduced in Greek city-states such as Athens in the late 6th century BC. Much as the Greeks liked it, it took quite a while for democracy to catch on. It was only in the 1700s that it really started to spread far and wide. Today, though, most nations have adopted this friendly form of government and many of those who haven't would like to.

Democracy: from the Greek *demos*, meaning "people," and *kratos*, meaning "power."

POWER TO
THE PEOPLE

Who rules?

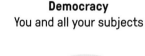

The main types of government

Autocracy
Just you

Monarchy
You and your family

Oligarchy
You and your family and/or friends

Democracy
You and all your subjects

Leading questions

Which form of government should you opt for?
Choose your preferred answers to these
questions and add up your scores to find out.

1. Do you like to boss people around?
a. Shut up and bring me my crown!
b. Just my little brother/sister.
c. No. Everyone else is scarier than me.

2. Are you confident in your own abilities?
a. Absolutely.
b. Sort of.
c. Ooh, I don't know.

3. Do you like sharing?
a. No way!
b. Happy to.
c. Here, have it all.

4. Are you a team player?
a. As long as I'm in charge.
b. Yes, let's do it!
c. Look, I'll just put my feet up while you lot
get on with it.

5. Are you happy to take responsibility?
a. I *said*: I'm in charge.
b. Only when I have to.
c. No! Whatever happened, it's not *my* fault!

How did you score?

a = 5 points, b = 3 points, c = 1 point

19–25 points:
You're not going to let go, are you? Stick
with autocracy for as long as you can.

11–18 points:
You need a little help from your friends.
Start with a monarchy or oligarchy.

5–10 points:
Get everyone involved. Opt for full democracy –
right now!

Second thoughts

Need some other options? Try:

Anocracy
A country where power is held by different elites that are competing with each other.

Theocracy
A country run by religious leaders on behalf of their god (modern examples are Vatican City and Iran).

Timocracy
A state in which only property owners can participate in government.

Hey!

Kleptocracy
A state run by leaders who are stealing from their subjects (okay, maybe forget this one).

Dicing with democracy

It's easy to see why democracy is popular. Citizens feel they have some influence on their government and, as a result, are usually happier about its decisions. There is, however, one important lesson that every aspiring leader should learn: even in a democracy, you can't please everyone all of the time.

Direct decisions

The simplest form of democracy is called direct democracy. This means everyone gets to vote on every issue. The micronation of Christiania in Denmark (see page 41) is run in this way. Every one of the citizens can attend Common Meetings, where new ideas and rules are debated and then decided by a vote. If you have only a small population, you can do the same.

On your behalf

But, really, who has time to attend every government meeting about every new law? Involving everyone all the time can also be complicated and pretty exhausting! So, not surprisingly, many micronations and most real nations opt for what's called representational government. That means citizens choose individuals to represent them in the nation's decision-making processes. In real countries, these representatives usually meet in a place known as a parliament.

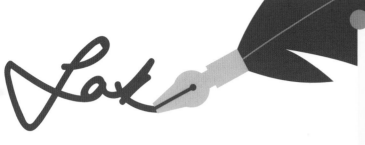

Concoct a constitution

A constitution is a document that sets out your country's form of government and its most important rules. For example, if you are determined that your citizens have certain rights or must do particular things (like bow to you every time they see you), put it in your constitution. Likewise, if you want to ban anything (slavery? homework? Brussels sprouts?), add that too. Write up your constitution and make sure you include the following:

1   The theme or principles of your country.

2   The most important rights your citizens will enjoy.

3   Your country's form of government.

4   A declaration that the constitution overrules other laws.

5   An explanation of how the constitution can be changed.

The long and the short of it

India has the world's longest constitution, consisting of 448 sections. The English translation runs to almost 120,000 words—roughly 480 pages. The shortest (but most famous) one is the U.S. constitution, with just seven sections and 4,400 words.

The world's oldest parliament is Iceland's. Known as the Althing ("General Assembly"), it was founded in 930.

Vote winning

To choose their representatives, people hold elections. You probably know how these work. Candidates present their ideas in speeches and pamphlets, shout slogans and do a lot of handshaking. People then vote for the candidate they like best. The one who gets the most votes is the winner.

Hold your own

If you've got enough people, you can hold your own elections. Why not start by having your citizens choose a prime minister or vice president to help you out? It should go something like this:

1. Encourage family, friends or anyone else you think will work hard for no money to stand for election.

2. Have them write documents or make speeches, saying why they should be elected. They could even invent their own political parties and make leaflets, posters and badges for their supporters to wear.

3. Make voting forms, known as ballot papers, and boxes into which voters can put their ballot papers.

4. On a particular day, get everyone to vote for their preferred candidate.

5. Add up the votes and declare a winner!

Wild parties

In true democracies, anyone can stand for election, to promote any kind of policy they want. That means there can be some strange candidates. In Britain, the Official Monster Raving Loony Party, whose main aim is to make fun of politics, has entered candidates in numerous elections since the 1980s and even won seats on some town councils.

POLLING PLACE

Free and fair

It's essential your elections are carefully organized to prevent any underhand tactics. So appoint one or more independent observers to monitor the process. They should check that all names on the ballot appear in the same format, that citizens vote only once and that all the votes are counted carefully. If there is any doubt about that last part, candidates can request a recount.

Rotten results

Throughout history some determined rulers have achieved remarkable election results by decidedly dodgy means. In Liberia, Africa, in 1927, Charles D. B. King managed to win 234,000 votes in a presidential election, even though there were only 15,000 registered voters in the country! His supporters had simply voted over and over again. And in 1962, Papa "Doc" Duvalier, president of Haiti, organized an election in which only his name appeared on the ballot. Not surprisingly, he won by a landslide, then declared himself president for life!

Staying in control

Elections are used to choose some heads of state, such as presidents. This is entirely admirable of course. But if you don't want to run the risk of losing control completely, a good option is to become what's known as a constitutional monarch.

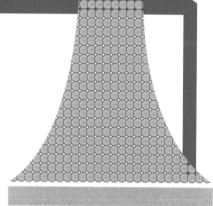

Keeping your hand in

As a constitutional monarch, you allow your subjects to choose the government but continue to be head of state, whether you are king or queen, emperor or empress. That way you still have a say in everything while graciously allowing democracy to take its course. Your citizens will be grateful and happy, and you will still rule. Or, thinking about it another way, others will get on with the hard work while you get to do all the fun stuff.

Modern monarchies

In the modern world, there are two types of constitutional monarchies. In so-called ceremonial ones, the monarch simply approves laws created by his or her government and does a lot of waving, nodding, and smiling at official ceremonies. In so-called executive ones, the monarch still gets to make the final decisions, throw a tantrum when they don't like something, and order everyone around. Which will you opt for?

Making your mark

As head of state, even in a democracy, you'll need to approve a lot of laws, declarations and proclamations. Simply sticking your initials or thumbprint at the bottom of a page really won't do. If you are a leader with style, you must have an official seal or stamp and a *really* cool signature.

Symbol of authority

From ancient times, rulers used seals to add a royal symbol to official documents. In the Middle Ages, monarchs wore seals in the form of rings, known as signet rings, which they used to make a sign in a circle of soft wax. Even today, many laws are made official by the addition of a royal or presidential seal.

Seal of approval

If you're crafty, you can make your own seal.

1. Take a small ball of air-dry clay and roll it into a cylinder. Flatten the end.

2. Inscribe your initials or national symbol in the flat clay. Remember the design has to be back to front, so that the printed image will be the right way round. Let the clay dry thoroughly.

3. When you need to approve a law or proclamation, ask one of your adult citizens (parents) to help you melt a blob of colored sealing wax onto the bottom of the document.

4. As you let the wax cool a little, rub your seal with cooking oil to prevent the wax sticking.

5. Press the seal into the soft wax, hold for 1–2 seconds, then remove carefully. Your initials or symbol will appear in the wax, which will then set hard.

A royal flourish

You'll also need to add your royal signature, so start practicing. Don't bother about keeping it small and neat—you're not at school now. Turn it into something bold and flashy. Get some big loops in there and finish off with some swishy underlining. It doesn't matter if you can actually read it, as long as it's grand and impressive. The important thing is that it looks like the autograph of a born leader.

Get down to business

6

For a country to prosper, it has to have money. You can start off by creating a currency for your citizens to use, but you'll also need to bring in money by making and selling things. Take a look around and see what you might have to offer.

Make money!

First, think up a name for your currency. Maybe it's the Kimlandian dollar, or the Jimmy, or the blong. Usually a currency is divided into smaller units, such as cents or pence. Perhaps 100 bings could make a blong?

Face value

Draw designs for banknotes of different values. Make sure you do both sides and incorporate a portrait of the country's glorious ruler—that's you! Other elements might include your national flag or coat of arms. If you draw your designs by hand, scan them and save them as a computer file. Then you can print out money whenever you need it—a handy thing for any ruler to be able to do!

Hard cash

You can make coins out of air-dry clay, using a round cookie-cutter. Print a design in the soft clay, perhaps using your official stamp (see page 59), and mark the denomination—10, 20, 50 bings?—on the back. The coins don't even have to be round—the Grand Duchy of Westarctica has issued an attractive series of square coins and even a triangular one.

Currencies of note

Many micronations have printed colorful banknotes and minted real coins. Some of these coins are made of precious metals such as gold or silver and, as a result, are much in demand among coin collectors (also called "numismatists"). Gold Celeston coins issued by the Nation of Celestial Space (page 18) in 1959–61 are now sold for around $1,000 each!

What's it worth?

A tricky part of developing a currency is agreeing what it is actually worth. One way to deal with that is to link your currency to another major currency.

So, for example, you can say your blong will always be worth one U.S. dollar or one U.K. pound. The currency of the micronation of the Principality of Seborga in Italy—which was founded in 1963, though it dates back to the 11th century—is the luigino. Each luigino is said, in Seborga, to be worth U.S.$6. It would be the most valuable currency in the world, if other countries accepted it!

Got enough dough?

Another way to put a value on your currency is to decide that it is worth, say, five minutes of anyone's labor, or the current price of an item. Many countries use the price of gold as their measure, but you could use something simpler, like the price of a particular candy bar from a particular store. If the price goes up, your currency is worth more; if it goes down, your currency is worth less. The Republic of Molossia's currency, the valora (divided into 100 futtrus), is linked to the current value of Pillsbury cookie dough, with roughly three valoras equalling one tube of dough.

Resource rich?

Some countries make most of their money from resources—natural things like land, timber and minerals such as oil and gold. How about you? Have you got fields and forests? Are there riches hidden in or under your land?

Flower power

You may not have room for acres of wheat or corn, but small crops of flowers can be profitable. The relatively small country of the Netherlands produces two-thirds of the world's flower exports, including, most famously, tulips. In the 1600s, its tulips were so much in demand that a single tulip bulb was worth the same as 12 acres (5 hectares) of land or ten times the salary of a skilled worker! On a smaller scale, the Principality of Hutt River in Australia (page 27) obtains a good deal of its income by selling native wildflowers. Get your green fingers busy and grow some flowers in your garden (or window box)!

Buried treasure

Poke around among rocks or along rivers and beaches and you might find some attractive stones you can polish and sell, or maybe some lovely shells. Strike gold and you may think you've hit the jackpot. The downside though is that your country could then be swamped. A gold strike is almost always followed by a gold rush, when people flood in to seek their fortune. So, if you do strike it rich, best keep it quiet!

Digging deep

You never know what might lie beneath your feet. Fossil fuels—deposits of coal, oil or gas buried deep underground — have made some countries vast fortunes, including some seemingly barren desert nations. As a result of its oil and gas reserves, the tiny Middle Eastern country of Qatar is, on a per person basis, the world's richest nation.

Fertile ground

Rocks coated with thick layers of bird poop would not seem like promising territory. But in the mid-1800s scientists discovered that bird poop was a rich source of a substance called phosphate, which was much in demand for making fertilizers. As a result, some tiny poop-covered islands off South America, Africa, and Arabia became, for a time, the most valuable lands on Earth.

Power up!

Can you make use of other natural resources? Could you harness the power of sunlight, wind or waves to make your own energy, for example? The island micronation of the Kingdom of North Dumpling, off the northeast coast of the United States, does just that. Using wind turbines, solar panels and low-energy lighting, its ruler and only resident, inventor Dean Kamen, has made his kingdom completely self-sufficient in electricity.

Making dough

If natural resources are in short supply, you and your citizens can make things to sell, or offer services that other people will be happy to pay for. Get some businesses going and let people know. Start small, but think big!

Sell your wares

Are you good at baking, sewing, pottery or woodworking? How about setting up a stall where you or some of your subjects offer your wares? You can sell them to other citizens or visitors from other countries. If your nation's businesses grow, they may need to pay more people to help them. And if visitors get excited about your products, they might ask you to send some to their country. Selling things to another country is called exporting, and the opposite—buying things from another country—is importing.

Lend a hand

Perhaps you can start a lawn-mowing, car-washing or dog-walking service and offer it to other citizens and neighboring nations. Many small countries with modest resources have specialized in offering useful services. In Luxembourg, for example (the world's only real Grand Duchy), they are always happy to look after other people's money and are very good at doing it. This has helped make Luxembourg the world's second richest country.

Managing the economy

As soon as your citizens start selling and buying from each other, your country has what's known as an economy. As ruler, you (or your government) have to decide whether you will keep control of the economy (a centralized economy) or just let it run itself (a free market). A bit of both seems to work best. Set some ground rules and then let people get on with it.

Taking a cut

You want to get something out of all this buying and selling, though, don't you? And you'll need it, to pay for all the things your citizens might come to expect as your country grows—healthcare, schools (really, they *will* want them), highways, cool bikeways and so on. One way for a ruler or government to take a cut from economic activity is to ask citizens to pay taxes. These might not make you popular, but they're almost always necessary.

Handing it over

You can decide when and how people should pay taxes. Usually, it's when they earn money—they hand over a small proportion of their pay as "income tax." But governments also make people pay taxes when they buy things (these are called sales taxes). For a ruler, the trick is to collect enough taxes to pay for nice things for everyone, without making people feel they are paying too much.

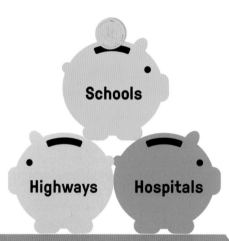

Tax havens

A few real countries have adopted another strategy when it comes to income tax: they ask for very little or even none at all. This attracts rich people who come to live in their country. Rich people tend to spend more, which boosts business and the government collects more in the form of sales taxes. Famous tax havens, as such places are known, include Monaco and the mountain microstate of Andorra (seen here).

National networks

High up on your list of things to spend your taxes on will be transport and communications. How are your people going to get around? And do they need rules to guide them and make your nation stand out from others?

Well-worn paths

Your new country might only have pathways rather than highways. Even so, you'll have to keep them clear and smarten them up every so often, and perhaps add some helpful signs so that people know where they are going. You'll also have to devise some traffic rules. Should people travel on the left side of the highway, for instance, as in Britain, Australia, India and a handful of other nations, or on the right, as in most countries?

Long hauls

Ask your citizens to use eco-friendly transport whenever possible. If your nation is tiny, that will be easy, as they will be able to walk everywhere. If it's a little bigger, encourage them to cycle. For long-distance travel, skip superhighways and build efficient railroads. Remarkably, the minuscule Republic of Molossia (page 44) has its own rail service. Hauled by stylish vintage locomotives, it links several parts of the republic. The fact that it is a tiny scale model does, however, make it all but impossible for passengers to board!

Measure up

People usually measure distances in miles or kilometers. But you could devise your own system of measurements. The Republic of Molossia's main unit is the Norton, which equals 7 inches or 17.7 centimeters—the length of the president's hand.

In your own time

To which time zone will you belong? The same one as adjacent nations, or one that's entirely your own? The island micronation of Elleore (page 11) has an official time 12 minutes ahead of nearby Copenhagen, Denmark's capital, while Ladonia (page 41) is three minutes behind neighbouring Sweden. Set *your* clocks now!

Centuries away

And why stop at a different hour? How about another century? The Empire of Atlantium (page 9) operates on a different calendar, the Annus Novus calendar. Each year is divided into ten months, and Annus Novus years are counted from 10,501 years before 1981—the year Atlantium was founded. So the year 2010 was the year 10,529 in Atlantium. Clear as mud? Good!

To the letter

Even in this era of email and instant messaging, we still send and receive goods in the mail. So it's a good idea to set up a national postal service. As many micronations have found, this can also be a good way to generate cash.

First post

Start with a couple of mailboxes. Have your postal workers gather the mail every day or two and then deliver it to the right addresses. People pay for postal services through taxes and by buying stamps. So it's a great idea to design your own stamps and sell them to your citizens.

POSTES

Early deliveries

People first used ink stamps to show that postage had been paid in the 1680s, in London. But stick-on paper stamps were not invented until 1840, when the British postal system issued the Penny Black. More than 68 million of these stamps were issued. Depending on its condition, a single Penny Black may be worth anything from $20 to $7,000 today!

Putting your stamp on it

1. Buy sheets of white adhesive paper.

2. Divide each sheet into small panels. Stamps are usually rectangular but can also be square or even triangular.

3. Draw or print a design on each stamp. Stamp designs often include national symbols or a portrait of the country's ruler, but can show landscapes or even wildlife.

4. Create stamps of different values: 10 bings, 50 bings, 1 blong?

5. Open a post office where you will sell the stamps.

1Blong

The word "post" originated in Persia. There, it meant "a message to which an answer is expected."

10Bi

50Bi

Face value

Making your own stamps doesn't cost much—just the price of some paper and ink. If you give them a decent value and sell plenty, you could make a handsome profit. What's more, the stamps of new nations are popular with tourists and stamp collectors (philatelists). Sell to those people too and you could soon be covering more than the costs of your postal service.

A small triumph

The Republic of Saugeais, a sizeable micronation founded in eastern France in 1947, is the only micronation to be featured on a real country's stamps. In 1987 the French postal service issued a stamp commemorating its historic sites and showing its coat of arms. That's almost official recognition!

REPUBLIQUE FRANÇAISE POSTES 1987 2.50 MONTBENOIT LE SAUGEAIS

Keep them coming

Crops, crafts, services, taxes, and stamps—they'll all help bring in funds.
But when it comes to making money, it's hard to beat tourism. So find more ways
to attract visitors and keep the tourist dollars, pounds and blongs rolling in.

Next!

Entry fee 10Bl

Show off
Offer guided tours of your nation, including viewings of major landmarks and historic sites. People like nothing better than mixing with royalty, so they might be willing to pay big bucks for an audience with the king or queen (yes, that's you). Make sure you offer them a cup of tea, too.

Star attractions
Can you create an eye-catching landmark? If it sparks interest, it could become a tourist attraction. In 1976, Alex Brackstone declared his farm in South Australia a separate nation, the Province of Bumbunga, and swore to remain loyal to the reigning British monarch, Queen Elizabeth II. He then created a colossal map of Britain—the size of several large fields—using strawberry plants. It attracted much attention in the media but, sadly, the plants died in a drought before the tourists flocked in.

Annual fixtures

Think about organizing regular events, such as music festivals, food fairs and sporting competitions, and invite people from other nations. The annual festival on the island kingdom of Elleore (page 11) includes the cleverly named Ellympics sporting competition and the Ellevision Song Contest.

Knowledge base

Have you or any of your citizens got special skills you could pass on to others? If so, you could offer courses or classes, as they do in the Free Republic of Alcatraz in Italy. Founded by Jacopo Fo in 2009 and located on a large countryside property, this micronation aims to develop a progressive, eco-friendly community—with a fondness for laughter and poetry. Visitors can take courses in cookery, gardening, yoga and more. The republic also has a hotel and a museum.

Worth a shot

Got any stunning scenery or quaint old buildings? If so, your country could be an ideal movie-making location. Movie companies will pay big bucks to shoot in particular places and if a film is successful it can give tourism a huge boost. That's certainly what New Zealand found after *The Lord of the Rings* and *The Hobbit* series of films were made there. Thousands of people now visit the country just to see where the films were shot—even though much of the action was created on computers!

7 Dress it up

People like nothing better than a bit of pomp and ceremony. It can do wonders for a leader's image and boost the tourist trade too. So jazz things up. Invent a few traditions. Devise some festivals and parades. In other words, put on a show!

Look the part

If you are going to win over and inspire your citizens, you've got to look like a leader. But what style will you choose? Consider your options and get working on your attire.

Royal regalia

Monarchies may be a little bit old-fashioned, but it's amazing how much people still love royal splendor and a bit of bling. If you opt for royal gear, you'll need a cloak, a crown and a scepter. Scour thrift shops for potential cloaks; look for velvet or silk-like material, ideally with fur trim. Crowns, however, can be trickier to come by. A plastic tiara could fool people into thinking it's the real thing, or else you could make a crown out of cardboard, paint it gold or wrap it in aluminum foil, and add some "jewels" (colored candy wrappers perhaps?). For a super simple scepter, stick a table tennis ball in the top of a cardboard tube and decorate in the same way. Remember to practice your royal wave!

Action wear

Do you want to look like a ruler who leads from the front? Then get into a uniform. Even some peaceable monarchs like to march around in uniforms, although they've often barely sighted a battlefield let alone fought in a war. Thrift shops often have old uniforms of one kind or another. If they are a bit plain, you can jazz them up by adding shiny buttons, pins, and medals and gold-foil stripes and epaulettes (those little straps on the shoulders). Ready? Quick march!

What's your style?

Take this test to find out how you should dress for public appearances.

What type of clothes do you prefer?
1. Wild outfits and dazzling colors.
2. Super stylish ones with designer labels.
3. I wear whatever my mom buys me.
4. I'm most comfortable in my scout uniform.

What do you say at the hair salon?
1. Dye it blue and gel it straight up.
2. Make me look like this fashion model.
3. Only a trim, I don't want anyone to notice.
4. Shave it all off. At once!

What's your attitude to fashion?
1. I have my own style — outrageous!
2. I always follow the latest styles.
3. I like to be smart but not stand out.
4. I think we should all dress the same — and have very shiny shoes!

How did you score?

Add up the numbers of your answers and check your overall style score:

3–4 points:
You're over the top and like to shock. Go royal, maybe a blend of punk and the style of 18th century French king Louis XIV, history's most outrageous royal dresser!

5–6 points:
You're a serious fashionista. Check out the latest paparazzi snaps of modern royals and track down their outfits. Be warned: they could be pricey.

7–10 points:
Play safe, smart, and sensible. Dress in suits. Make sure you have some bodyguards, though—otherwise you might go unnoticed in your own country.

11-12 points:
You've got discipline and a hard edge. Get into a uniform and start knocking everything and everyone into shape.

Get some culture

The people of a country are united by their homeland, their flags and laws and, of course, their love for their ruler. But they're also connected by their shared culture. That means their language, history, literature, art, songs, traditions, food, and national symbols. Can you conjure up a culture for your country?

Speak up

Languages take a long time to develop, but you can get things moving by inventing a few words and phrases. Start with some simple greetings your citizens can use when they meet. In the Aerican Empire (page 31), the traditional greeting is "Plod!," while "Soussan?" means "How are you?". Talossa (page 9) has its own complete language, and a dictionary containing more than 28,000 Talossan words! You might also come up with other signs of greeting such as a particular kind of salute or wave. Aericans hold up their right hand with the index and middle finger raised like rabbit ears and waggle them from side to side.

Team mascots

People like to be part of a team. To show it, they wear team colors and pins. You've already got your flag and coat of arms, but you can also choose other national symbols, such as a national plant, fruit, bird or other animal. And if nothing real seems suitable, you can always invent something. North Korea's national animal is the *chollima*, a mythical winged horse that can supposedly fly hundreds of miles a day.

Game on!

If you and your people are a sporty bunch, you can also nominate a national sport. Is there one you're all really keen on? Or can you invent an entirely new sport? Elleore (page 11) has a national sport called cracket, while the Aerican Empire has one called sillyball. At least if you make up your own sport, you're almost assured to be the best at it!

Country cooking

Food is something else that marks out a country. Italians have their pasta, for example, Americans their hamburgers and Indians their spicy curries. Have you got a favorite dish you want to declare your national food? Or can you whip something up in the kitchen? It could even just be a national sandwich—the Kimlandian double-decker, perhaps? Whatever you concoct, make sure it's easy to make—and that your citizens like it, as they'll be eating it a lot!

Wear it well

Wearing a national costume is part of everyday life in some countries—many Indian women dress daily in long robes called saris, for example, and the Japanese can be seen relaxing in their bathrobe-like kimonos. A national costume can also be a way to display pride in your country on special occasions—think of the Scots and their kilts. Okay, so a kilt might not be for everyone, but you can no doubt come up with something dashing, distinctive and, hopefully, comfortable for your citizens to strut around in. Sketch it out on paper and try to include some distinctive features like national colors and symbols.

History in the making

Since you've only just started, you might be a bit short of history. But perhaps you can delve deeper into the past to chronicle the ancient origins of your country and its people. Many nations have much-loved stories of legendary heroes and fantastical creatures that once roamed their land. See what you can dig up, or dream up using your vivid imagination. Be a myth-maker!

Sing your country

There's nothing better than a song to get people all emotional and misty-eyed about a country—whether they live there or not. So compose some catchy tunes with inspiring lyrics and get everybody singing along.

All together now

Top of your playlist should be a national anthem—a song that proclaims what a wonderful nation you live in and how terrific its ruler is. Write some lyrics that express what you want your citizens to feel for their country. Be bold: urge your people to celebrate and look forward to an exciting future. Use this example to help you get started. Fill in the blanks and then pick your favorite of the options.

O citizens of _____ , rise up/unite/hear the call!
Beloved compatriots/Courageous comrades/
Sons and daughters of our noble kingdom/empire,
We will honour our beautiful country
and its children all,
We will fight to protect its lands/
defeat tyrants and invaders/drive off annoying
siblings and nosy neighbors.
We are united in our love of freedom, our homeland
and our great leader _____ /our loathing of
tyranny, homework and Brussels sprouts.
Come, sing of our land of beauty/
the land of our heart's desire,
Together we celebrate our shining future/
our glorious destiny
etc etc.

Stirring sounds

If you're musical, you might also manage to compose an appropriate tune. Remember: it needs to be grand and stirring, with some big, bombastic sounds, like trumpet fanfares and drum rolls, but it's also got to be easy to sing along to.

Lend me your anthem

Maybe music's not your thing? In that case, just borrow a tune and match your lyrics to it. Several micronational anthems use the melody of *God Save the Queen*, the national anthem of the United Kingdom. But perhaps you could put your own spin on it and use your favorite modern rock tune.

Star power

The national anthem of the Principality of Hutt River (page 27) was written by an Australian pop band, Jon English and the Foster Brothers, in 1983, after Prince Leonard met them on a TV show. The lyrics go as follows:

It's a hard land but it's our own land
Built with love and dedication
Self-assured is our small nation
One man's dream of independence
God bless the Prince of The Hutt River Province
God bless the man whose dream has come true

Miss and hit

The Republic of Saugeais (page 69) released its national anthem on a vinyl record. Sadly, it failed to show up on the French charts. It did, however, make it onto a 2013 CD compilation called *The Complete National Anthems of the World*, which also features the national anthems of Hutt River, Sealand and Seborga. Check it out—it's a must for all aspiring rulers!

Songs of longing

You should also write songs about your country's history, myths and heroes, not to mention its beautiful landscapes and warm-hearted people. Songs of this type tend to be particularly popular with citizens travelling or living abroad. That's because they express the sense of sadness and longing these poor people feel as soon as they leave their marvelous homeland. Get them singing and they'll soon be back!

Time out

Give your people a break now and then—plan some national public holidays. Your citizens will be delighted to have some time off work or school, and all the more ready to celebrate their nation and show their gratitude to you.

Back to the start

The most important day of your nation's year should be its foundation day or independence day. That's the day you set up your country or declared it independent from another country. Make it a public holiday and a huge celebration. Prepare music and flags and get everyone to dress up in national costume. If you have enough citizens, ask them to make floats and organize a parade for you to watch from a suitably royal vantage point.

Birthday bash

Look for other opportunities for a day off and a national celebration. Often, countries have a public holiday to mark the birthday of their ruler. Sounds like a great idea, doesn't it? That way you get an even bigger party and even more presents.

Red-letter days

You can also use holidays to honour a favorite family member or pet, mark other memorable achievements in the history of your nation, or celebrate events in the wider world that might inspire your people. True to its spirit of silliness, the Aerican Empire (page 31) has some bizarre national days, including Oops Day, on 27 February—supposedly the day on which Italy's Tower of Pisa tilted and all at once became the famous Leaning Tower of Pisa.

Once-a-year war

An annual event might be used to remind people why your country was founded in the first place. After the U.S. city of Annapolis closed a bridge leading to the waterside district of Eastport, people there decided to form an independent state, the Maritime Republic of Eastport. Today its most famous annual celebration is the Tug of War in November—also known as the Slaughter across the Water—between Eastport and Annapolis. Teams of people on either side pull on a 1,640ft. (500m) rope stretched across the water between the two districts— until one side gives way!

Play time

Another option is to have a holiday so that you can all participate in a group activity. Choose something crazy and you'll give your citizens a good laugh *and* pull the tourists in. These might give you some ideas:

- India's Holi festival (March), when people all over the country fling handfuls of colored powder at each other.
- Thailand's Songkran festival (April), when Thais throw and spray water at each other until everyone is soaked. It's a blast!
- South Korea's Boryeong mud festival (July), when locals and thousands of tourists roll around in thick, soft mud.
- Spain's Tomatina festival in Buñol, Valencia (August), when people pelt each other with mushy tomatoes.

Yikes!

In 2013 the government of Peru announced that National Guinea Pig Day would from then on be held every October. Unfortunately for guinea pigs, the event celebrates their usefulness as a tasty snack rather than as a cuddly pet.

8

Troubleshooting

Running a country isn't all parties, parades and singalongs. Sometimes things can get a bit messed up. Storms strike, citizens start grumbling or fighting, the neighbors turn on you … Best be prepared.

National security

A good ruler ensures the safety of his or her people, maintains law and order, and seeks to improve the lives of the country's population. Are you doing enough to keep your citizens safe and happy?

Your rules

Whatever laws you've established, someone will always break them. As ruler, you've got to decide how to deal with this. Can you handle it yourself, or do you need a police force? How do you punish law-breakers?
You could give fines or have offenders do community service—work for the country for free for a period of time. If you need a stronger punishment, you can threaten to cancel their citizenship and banish them from your realm. The thought of leaving your wonderful country will soon bring them to their senses.

Novel approach

Some micronations have unusual rules—and punishments. As an island that enjoys its isolation, Elleore (page 11) is not fond of the novel *Robinson Crusoe*, which, it feels, gives a "distorted and false impression of how life is on a small island." Anyone caught bringing the book to Elleore is punished harshly, by being sent to a nearby "jail island" for a soul-destroying 11 minutes and 17 seconds. That soon sorts them out!

EXILE

Take the happiness test

As ruler, you've got to try to work out what will make your people happy. You might pick up some tips from a tool created by an important international body, the Organization for Economic Development. It's called the Better Life Index and it lists 11 things that have been shown to make citizens happy. Give yourself a check mark or a cross against each issue and add up your score to find out how you are doing.

Hazard watch

Wherever you are, you are seldom safe from extreme weather such as storms. And then there are other potential threats, like power cuts, food shortages or interfering parents. Plan ahead to protect your citizens. Organize an emergency response team. Stockpile snacks in case the weather is so bad you can't make it to the shops or your dad grounds you for a week (potentially a devastating blow for any ruler).

☐ **Safety:** That means your people feel safe and secure. You'll be working on this now. Got it sorted yet?

☐ **Housing:** You might be living in luxury in your palace or throne room, but do your citizens have nice homes?

☐ **Jobs:** Work can be a source of satisfaction. Are you keeping everyone busy?

☐ **Income:** Money may not buy happiness, but it sure helps. Are your businesses booming?

☐ **Community:** Do your people like to hang out together and have fun? Or do you need more games and parties to bring them together?

☐ **Education:** Smart citizens tend to create a safer, healthier, wealthier nation. Are your people top of the class?

☐ **Environment:** Nice surroundings, in other words. No doubt you picked a cool place for your country, but are you keeping it tidy and unspoiled?

☐ **Civic engagement:** That means having a say in running your country. Can your citizens vote?

☐ **Health:** You know what they say: if you haven't got your health, you haven't got anything. Are you keeping your nation fit?

☐ **Work-life balance:** People won't want to work all the time. Have you got enough holidays?

☐ **Life satisfaction:** Are your citizens a happy bunch? Do they seem satisfied with life in your country?

Happiness score?

1–3 Oh dear. Have you really been paying attention? Turn to chapter 1 and start again.

4–6 Time to smarten up—before there's a revolution.

7–9 Excellent progress. Just review your current policies and see where you can make things *even* better.

10–11 Can we move in?

Love thy neighbor?

You'll do your best to get on with everyone, of course. But we all have disagreements now and then, and countries are no different. Try to make the best of difficult situations and keep other nations onside. If all else fails, though, you need to be ready to stand up for yourself!

Border flashpoints

If you do clash with a neighboring nation, aim to resolve disputes peacefully. Meet with the other country's ruler, or have your representatives (called ambassadors) get together. If necessary, write up an agreement saying how you have decided to settle the dispute. That might involve redrawing boundaries or one country offering compensation for any damage. You may just have to swallow your pride and pay for that broken window!

Third party

If the two sides can't get along, ask someone from a different country—another ruler, lawmaker or any sensible adult—to help settle the dispute. This strategy, known as arbitration, is often used by real nations, and the third party is usually another country or an international organization such as the United Nations (see page 37). Get talking!

Agreeing to disagree

Sometimes neither side will give an inch and an argument goes on and on. For instance, since 1984, India and Pakistan have quarreled and occasionally done battle over the exact location of the border between the two countries on the Siachen Glacier, in the mountains of Kashmir. It's a standoff that has cost each country a fortune and many lives. Don't let your disagreements drag on.

Standing firm

Should neighbors become aggressive, you have to stand your ground, even against the biggest bullies. The people of the Conch Republic (page 22) demonstrated that in September 1995, when the U.S. Army decided to conduct training exercises on their territory—without asking permission! The Conchs rebelled. They blocked the U.S. army and prepared to employ their most powerful weapons—water cannons and loaves of stale bread. Eager to avert all-out war, the U.S. Army battalion agreed to apologize, and was then allowed to pass through peacefully.

Swift response

Of course, if you try to grab someone else's territory, you can expect them to fight back. In 1971, U.S. businessman Michael Oliver claimed a tiny coral reef in the South Pacific Ocean and named it the Republic of Minerva. Oliver designed a flag, issued a currency and began planning to extend the islands by piling sand on them. But the nearby nation of Tonga had other ideas. The Tongan king, his ministers, a brass band, and a platoon of soldiers sailed to the reef and proclaimed its ownership of the reefs. In 1972 this claim was recognized by other nations and that was it for poor Mr Oliver and his Republic.

You and whose army?

With the risk of international conflict seemingly ever-present, it's worth thinking more about your defenses. Is your nation safe? Do you need higher fences, better security, or even a real army?

HAVE YOUR PERMITS READY FOR INSPECTION

SECURE COMPOUND

On guard

A new fledgling nation like yours may not need massed ranks of soldiers, but you might still want to appoint one or two family members or friends to take charge of your security. They can keep an eye on your borders for you and, if there's any sign of danger, issue alerts to citizens. Give your commanders uniforms or at least official-looking caps or armbands, so that people know who they are. Teach them how to salute and shout orders.

Badge of honour

Encourage acts of bravery and heroism by awarding military honors—medals, in other words. You can make them by decorating disks of gold or silver cardboard and attaching them to ribbons. Famous and important military honors include the U.S. Purple Heart and Britain's Victoria Cross. Give your medals striking names like these—the Kimlandian Cross, perhaps, or the Gold Star of Alexistan?

They shall not pass

You might pick up some military tips from the historic micronation of Seborga in Italy (page 61). Its impressive official guard wear smart blue uniforms, watch over the Prince of Seborga and his family, and man a sentry post at the entrance to the state. Despite the total force numbering no more than two or three at any one time, it is clearly highly effective, as no one has invaded for centuries.

Sea power

Got a boat and some water to run it on? Then maybe you could have a naval force too. Even though it lies far from the sea, in an area of desert, the tiny micronation of Molossia has its own navy, consisting of one rubber dinghy, the *MS Wombat*.

Token force

Of course, if you're far enough away from everyone else you might not have to worry. Iceland, in the north Atlantic Ocean, has no full-time army and just a small group of military personnel and reserves. Other countries with no full-time army include Andorra, Costa Rica, Liechtenstein and the remote Pacific island states of Nauru, Palau and Tuvalu.

I'll scratch your back

Of course it's far better to make friends rather than war. Do another country a good turn and it's likely to return the favor. Do it some more and you'll end up with a bunch of friendly nations—otherwise known as allies.

Side by side

Countries often make agreements to support each other. Sometimes they agree to sell their goods and services to each other and allow their citizens to move freely between their countries. Nations also agree to back each other in the event of war. NATO, or the North Atlantic Treaty Organization, is an alliance of 28 North American and European nations who have promised to protect each other and keep the peace. Do any of your friends have their own countries? If not, show them this book at once and get them to create their own country so that you can form your first alliance!

Islands of influence

Most real nations and some micronations have taken the smart step of setting up offices in other countries. These are known as "embassies" if they are large offices with ambassadors present or "consulates" if they are smaller setups. Having an embassy or consulate promotes good relations with the host nation and provides support to any of your citizens who may be passing through that country. If you have good friends abroad, perhaps they could agree to set up an embassy or consulate for your new nation where they live.

Join the club

Real countries have formed organizations to discuss international issues, such as the United Nations (page 37). Micronations have followed suit by creating what could be called intermicronational groups (say that five times fast!). Polination is a conference held every two or three years to bring together micronational leaders to hang out with other rulers, compare uniforms and swap ideas. So far it has been held in London, U.K.; Sydney, Australia; and Perugia in Italy.

Just for fun

There are also less formal ways for countries to get together and promote good relations. Sport, for example. Why not get a few friendly nations together and have your own sporting championships or even a micronational Olympics?

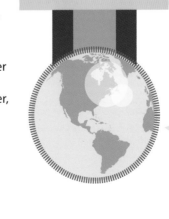

Best behavior

While sashaying across the world stage as the leader of a new nation, you should always be careful to set a good example to other countries and aspiring rulers. Treat your people well. Make friends with other countries and help them out. And do your bit to find solutions to global problems, such as poverty, hunger, pollution and global warming. You may be the big shot in your own nation, but you're also a citizen of the world.

GLOBAL CITIZEN

WORLD LEADER

9 Pass it on

All good things come to an end, right? At some point, you may not want to carry on as leader, or you may feel you are losing your grip on power. That's why it's important to consider your legacy—who will follow you and how you'll be remembered.

Preparing the way

You might not feel ready to give up the throne just yet, but it's a good idea to start thinking about succession—who will take over after you. Older rulers may already have their children waiting in the wings, but you won't have that option just yet. However, you can still appoint a trusted friend or relative to continue your good work, or you could allow your subjects to elect a new leader.

A matter of timing
In many ways, it's a good idea to carry out the handover while you are still in charge. That will allow you to select your successor, give the new boy or girl some good advice, and make sure it's all running smoothly before you chill out. Make sure, though, that you put the change in writing, have your citizens agree with it and make it official. Then it's less likely that people will fight or ignore your wishes.

Now you see them

If your favored successor is still very young you might want to appoint what's known as a regent. This is an older person who will help your successor rule until they are big enough to do it themselves. But make sure your regent is trustworthy. Throughout history, regents have swiftly elbowed their charges out of the way and snatched power themselves. Famously, the sons of King Edward IV of England, Edward and Richard, aged 12 and 9, were left in the care of their uncle, Richard of Gloucester, after their father's death in 1483. Richard locked the boys up in the Tower of London, while he made himself king. To this day, no one knows what happened to the princes.

Broken chain

Make sure you have the agreement of key people. If not, your plans could come to nothing. In 2005, Robert Ben Madison, founder of the micronation of Talossa (page 9) decided to abdicate—give up the throne—in favor of his wife's grandson, then eight years old, who became King Louis I. But Louis's mom wasn't entirely happy about her son becoming a king and had him abdicate in November 2006. This left the throne vacant until the following year, when Talossan citizen John Woolley was elected as King John I—not what Madison had intended.

Wars of succession

Probably the worst thing you can do is to do nothing. Depart without appointing a successor and there could be a mad scramble for power, fights and, if history is anything to go by, all-out war! The death of Henry I of England in 1135, for instance, left the throne vacant and resulted in a 19-year period of chaos and bloodshed known as The Anarchy. So make sure you have an efficient and peaceful handover—otherwise all your hard work could swiftly be wrecked!

All thanks to you!

How strong your legacy is depends on other people—the citizens of your nation. Make your citizens happy—or convince them you've made them happy—and you'll be commemorated in flags, banners, stories and monuments. You'll earn endless adulation and come as close as you can to achieving the impossible: immortality!

Smiling reminders

It's a good idea to make sure that, even once you are gone, your people will find it hard to forget you. So, while you still rule, get your face on all your coins and stamps. Have buildings, streets and other places named after you. Hang your portrait in prominent places around your country—on main streets, in shopping malls, and in the hallways of your house!

For the record

Insist that people know and read your side of the story. Compile a history of your country. Play up your heroic role in its founding and development, its successes and triumphs (skip the slip-ups and catastrophes). Illustrate it with photos of you leading the way, greeting other rulers and being acclaimed by your people. Distribute copies to your subjects, have it sold in shops and studied in schools. Make sure it's a bestseller in your country!

Set in stone

For something even more eye-catching and enduring, commission a magnificent monument to commemorate your glorious rule. Ideally it should be a life-size statue or model of you looking noble in royal robes or dashing in a military uniform, perhaps brandishing a sword as you courageously control a rearing horse (or wobbly bicycle). But if that's too challenging you can build something simpler and plonk it in your yard or another prominent part of your country. Perhaps it could be a heroic figure made of tin cans, or a mini-pyramid built of stones or bricks (well, it worked for the ancient Egyptian pharaohs!).

Standing out

You could follow the example of ancient Roman emperors and have someone make you a memorial column. Trajan's Column in Rome was built to honour the Emperor Trajan and completed in AD 113. It's more than 126ft. (36m) tall and decorated with carvings showing Trajan's military triumphs. Located in a busy street, it reminds passersby what a great guy Trajan was—nearly 2,000 years after he died. Nice one, Trajan!

Rock solid

After a while, though, people tend not to notice statues and columns. So perhaps you need to think even bigger, and find something that will really stop people in their tracks every time. How about an entire mountain carved into the shape of you? In South Dakota, USA, the heads of four great U.S. presidents—George Washington, Thomas Jefferson, Theodore Roosevelt, and Abraham Lincoln—were chiseled out of the face of Mount Rushmore by sculptor Gutzon Borglum. Each head is as tall as a six-storey building. No one overlooks that!

A wiser way

And yet … statues can be toppled, monuments torn down, even mountains reshaped or blown up (it has happened). Perhaps a much better, simpler, and cheaper way to glory is just to win your people's hearts. Rule right—fairly and wisely—and they will be eternally grateful. They'll tell inspiring tales about their leader, and their stories and their love for you will be passed on to future generations. That way, your name and fame will live on through the ages. And, in your people's eyes at least, you will rule … forever!

Glossary

autocracy A country ruled by one person

border A line that divides one country or region from another

capital The city where a country's government is located

citizen An inhabitant of a country who is allowed to live there permanently and is protected by that country

constitution A document that describes a country's most important laws and its form of government

country An area of land that is separated from other places by borders and has a population and its own government

currency The type of money used by a country

democracy A country in which the citizens elect their government

duchy A country ruled by a duke or duchess

economy The making, buying, and selling of goods and services

empire A country ruled by an emperor or empress

federation A country made up of a group of states or regions, each with its own government

government The group of people or system that runs a country

independent Free to make decisions and rules, without the approval of anyone else

kingdom A country ruled by a king or queen

micronation A made-up country that is not recognized by real countries

microstate A very small real country

monarch A ruler, such as a king, queen or emperor, whose position is passed to their children after their death

monarchy A country ruled by a monarch

nation A country; or, more precisely, a group of people who share the same language and culture

oligarchy A country ruled by a small group of people

parliament A place where members of some governments meet

passport A document issued by a country, which lets its citizens into other countries

population The people of a country

principality A country ruled by a prince or princess

republic A country ruled by an elected president

secede To separate from another country and become independent

tax Money citizens pay to their government to help run their country

territory Land that belongs to a country

United Nations An international organization formed to help countries work together

virtual nation A country that exists only online

Index

A

Aerican Empire	31, 74–5, 78
Ahzivland, State of	39
Alcatraz, Free Republic of	71
allies	86–7
ambassadors	82
anocracy	53
arbitration	82
armies	84–5
Atlantium, Empire of	9, 67
autocracy	48, 93

B

banknotes	60–1
Better Life Index	81
borders	20–5, 27, 82–4, 93
buffer zones	24
Bumbunga, Province of	70

C

calendars	67
capitals	46, 93
Caroline	10
Celestial Space, Nation of	18, 37, 61
ceremonies	34–5, 42, 58, 72–3, 78
checkpoints	22, 25
Christiania, Freetown of	41, 54
coats of arms	32, 60, 69, 74
coins	60–1, 90
Conch Republic	22, 83
constitutions	55, 58, 93
consulates	86
Copeman Empire	16
costumes	75, 78
culture	74–5
currency	60–1, 93

D

democracy	51, 54–5, 57–9, 93

E

Eastport, Maritime Republic of	79
economy	65, 93
elections	56–8
Elgaland-Vargaland, Kingdoms of	24
Elleore, Kingdom of	11, 67, 71, 75, 80
embassies	86
enclaves	25
exports/imports	64

F

festivals	79
flags	30–1, 34, 37, 39, 60, 74, 78, 90
Flandrensis, Grand Duchy of	13
food	75
Forvik, Sovereign State of	13, 33
frontiers	20–1
future generations	92

G

Google Maps	27
grids	26

H

heraldry	32
Hutt River	27, 62, 77

I

islands	10–11

K

kleptocracy	53
Koronis	18

L

Ladonia	41, 67
land grabs	9, 12–13
languages	74
leaders	48–54, 59, 87–9, 92
legacy	88, 90–1

M

map-making	26–7, 47
Marie Byrd Land	12–13
mascots	74
measurements	67
medals	84
Middle Earth	19
migration	40–1
Minerva, Republic of	83
Molossia, Republic of	44, 61, 66–7, 85
monarchy	50, 58, 72, 93
money	60–1
monuments	90–2

N

names	28–9
Naminara Republic	43
national anthems	76–7
New Atlantis	17
no-man's-land	24
North Dumpling, Kingdom of	63
North Sudan, Kingdom of	12

O

oligarchy	50, 93

P

parliaments	54–5, 93
passports	17, 22, 24, 39, 42–3, 93
photobombing	39

police	80
population	36, 38–47, 93
post	68–9
public holidays	78–9
punishments	80

R

Redonda, Kingdom of	10
resources	62–4

S

Saugeais, Republic of	69, 77
Sealand, Principality of	17, 77
Seasteading Institute	17
Seborga, Principality of	61, 77, 85
security	22–3, 80–1, 84–5
songs	76–7
sports	75, 87
stamps	68–9, 90
successors	88–9
surveyors	21
symbols	31–3, 59

T

Talossa	9, 13, 33, 74, 89
tax	65–6, 68, 93
theocracy	53
time zones	67
timocracy	53
tourists	22, 27, 39, 41, 43, 69–72, 79
transport	66
tyrants	48–9

U

uniforms	72–3, 84–5, 87, 91
United Nations (UN)	37, 82, 87, 93

V

virtual nations	19, 93

W

weather	81
websites	8, 22, 38, 41
Westarctica, Grand Duchy of	13, 60
Whangamomona, Republic of	50
Wirtland	19

Acknowledgements

Publishing Director	Piers Pickard
Commissioning Editor	Jen Feroze
Author	Scott Forbes
Illustrator	Emma Jones
Designer	Emma Jones
In-house Senior Designer	Andy Mansfield
Image Researcher	Shweta Andrews
Print production	Larissa Frost, Nigel Longuet

Thanks to:	Mina Patria, Sue McMillan, Caroline Hamilton, Lyahna Spencer

Lonely Planet Offices

Australia

90 Maribyrnong St, Footscray, Victoria, 3011, Australia
Phone: 03 8379 8000 Email: talk2us@lonelyplanet.com.au

USA

150 Linden St, Oakland, CA 94607
Phone: 510 250 6400 Email: info@lonelyplanet.com

United Kingdom

240 Blackfriars Road, London, SE1 8NW
Phone: 020 3771 5100 Email: go@lonelyplanet.co.uk

Published in September 2015 by Lonely Planet Publications Pty Ltd
ABN 36 005 607 983
www.lonelyplanetkids.com
© Lonely Planet 2015
© Photographs as indicated 2015
Printed in China

Photo credits

KEY: t -top, tc-top center, tr-top right, tl-top left, tcr- top center right, c-center, cr-center right, cl-center left, ca-center above, cb-center below, cla-center left above, clb- center left below, crb – center right below, b-bottom, bc-bottom center, br-bottom right, bl-bottom left.

Alamy: Hemis 27B; Nordicphotos 55C; Guy Bell 57T; REDA &CO sr 61C; PCJones 85B.
Flickr: Creative Commons 54B, 58C.
Getty Images: Anna Gorin 71B; Don McGillis 25C; Handout 83TC; Kurita Kaku 50CL; LPI Kimberley Coole 75TR; LPI Alfredo Maiquez 65B; LPI John Freeman 78B; LPI Richard I'Anson 47B; LPI Seongjoon Cho 43B; Manfred Gottschalk 20C; Stefan Cioata 29T; Visions Of Our Land 14C; Wallace Kirkland 37CR.
iStock: Lya Cattel 37TC; Neneos 53TR.
Lars Vilks: 41T.
Léo Delafontaine: 87T.
Lonely Planet: Akash Ghosh 79CL; Alexander Howard 91B.
Republic of Molossia: His Excellency President Kevin Baugh 61TR, 61TRB, 61BL, 61BR, 66CR.
Republic of Saugeais: 77C.
Wikipedia: Creative Commons Attribution-Share Alike 3.0 Unported license 9CR, 10B; Public Domain 9TC, 32BR, 33TC, 61T, 61TR, 63CR, 68CR, 73CR, 89T.
Wikitimbres: 69B.